CW00393518

PRISONERS OF THE EMPEROR

Ian

Prisoners of the Emperor

IAN MITCHELL

The Pentland Press
Edinburgh – Cambridge – Durham – USA

First published in 1996 by
The Pentland Press Ltd
1 Hutton Close
South Church
Bishop Auckland
Durham

ISBN 1-85821-409-2

Typeset by Carnegie Publishing, 18 Maynard St, Preston
Printed and bound by Antony Rowe Ltd, Chippenham

Contents

	Introduction	1
1	Surrender and Changi	5
2	River Valley Road Camp	21
3	To Thailand, Ban Pong, Wampo	55
4	Chungkai	103
5	Tamuang	141
6	Wampo-Tavoy Road	167
7	Tamuang, Bangkok, Takli, and Freedom	211
	Epilogue	229

Introduction

IN THIS BOOK Ian Mitchell has succeeded admirably in conveying to readers the unpredictable nature of life as a prisoner of war of the Japanese. I am honoured to be asked to contribute an introduction to his story which he recounts with clarity, dignity and humour.

Ian was only seventeen when Singapore capitulated to the Japanese on 15 February 1942 and he subsequently became one of the youngest Allied prisoners of war at Changi. Ian's brother, Ron, was his mainstay as a POW. Theirs was a Singapore-based family – their father was employed in the Public Works Department – but they were more fortunate than many in that the womenfolk escaped. Ian himself knew shortly after he was captured that his mother and sister had arrived safely in India. His father meanwhile was a civilian internee in Changi Jail.

Ian had joined the Straits Settlements Volunteer Force (SSVF) after leaving school, and though his military career as a dispatch-rider was brief, the camaraderie of this unit of amateur soldiers stood him in good stead throughout the three and a half years of his imprisonment. Ian depicts clearly how survival as a POW depended on the support of a small group of friends and how his own group evolved together with the moral code which governed it.

At working camps in Singapore town, Ian and his friends were quick to exploit their local knowledge; they were accustomed to the climate, the food and the customs, and could speak Malay.

He describes how their skills in outwitting the Japanese were honed. Ian also reminds his readers of the tragedy of the civilian population of 'Fortress' Singapore, particularly those Chinese who had taken up arms with the British and upon whom the full vengeance of the Japanese descended. He records a poignant conversation with an SSVF chaplain, Captain Parr, who had recognised among the bodies of Chinese executed on the beach at Changi a fellow pupil of Ian at St Andrew's School.

In October 1942 Ian was transported to Thailand to help construct the Burma-Thailand railway. There he experienced the hunger, fatigue, sickness and brutality associated with that infamous project. At the jungle camp at Wampo he found himself with his brother and his SSVF comrades within a larger group of three battalions commanded by one of the outstanding British POW camp commanders, Lieutenant-Colonel H.H. Lilly. The Japanese officer, Lieutenant Hattori Hiroshi, was content to leave much of the camp administration to Lilly and his staff so that for a few months Wampo was possibly the best run of the jungle camps on the River Kwai. Ian was fortunate too in his battalion medical officer, Captain S.S. Pavillard, whose innovative approach to jungle surgery and capacity for taking huge risks to secure drugs has ensured his legendary reputation in the history of the railway.

In early 1943 Ian fell critically ill with amoebic dysentery and was evacuated from the jungle camp to Chungkai, a POW 'hospital' camp in central Thailand. Although he missed the worst excesses of the Japanese determination to push through the railway regardless of the human cost, he was nevertheless separated from his group, even fearing that his brother had died. At Chungkai, Ian survived because the medical officer, in apportioning the minute quantity of emetine available, decided that Ian stood a chance of pulling through. His two neighbours in the hut were not so fortunate. Later, Ian was able to piece together the story of how the emetine was smuggled into the POW camps by men of his own unit.

Ian has the ability to convey to the reader the complete vacuum in which the average POW lived. He shows how the camps fed on rumour, the POWs surviving in a permanent state of uncertainty as to the intentions of their captors. Life was lived one day at a time. At Tamuang camp, where Ian spent most of 1944 in the company once more of his brother and his friends, he was suddenly ordered to join a working party making a road into Burma. This entailed a dramatic ride over the railway viaduct at Wampo, an extraordinary contraption of unseasoned timber which Ian well knew the POWs had done their best to sabotage during the construction. When peace was announced in August 1945, the POWs were apprehensive, fearing that this was just one more of the many false dawns which had occurred throughout their captivity.

Sibylla Jane Flower

Historian Sibylla Jane Flower, daughter of Lieutenant-Colonel Flower who commanded the 9th Northumberland Fusiliers throughout captivity in Singapore and Thailand, is writing a history of the Allied POWs of the Japanese.

CHAPTER I

Surrender and Changi

IT WAS 6 P.M. on Sunday 15 February 1942, in the garden of a suburban house in Singapore, when the platoon, assembled before Captain Holiday, was informed that Singapore had surrendered. They were prisoners of war. The terms of surrender required all arms and equipment to be handed over intact; failure to abide by the surrender terms would result in the offender being executed. The soldiers were told that a named warrant officer would immediately take over and be responsible for receiving their small arms for surrender to the Japanese.

The warrant officer took over. He was a much disliked person who had done a great deal more than his fair share of bullying and threatening the younger members of the platoon. More than once he had been promised that he would be 'shot up the arse' as soon as a suitable confused fighting situation permitted, and now, despite the circumstances of the occasion, the unpleasant bully was at it again. Having successfully arranged the collection of revolvers and their ammunition, he shouted his instructions for the unloading of rifles. Silently the soldiers commenced removing the magazines from their rifles and the rounds from the breech of each weapon. The final act of unloading was to point the weapon upwards and pull the trigger to show that the barrel was cleared and the gun was safe. Some in the platoon were very young and scarcely trained, if trained at all, and their slowness provided another opportunity for the warrant officer to be unpleasantly aggressive and demanding.

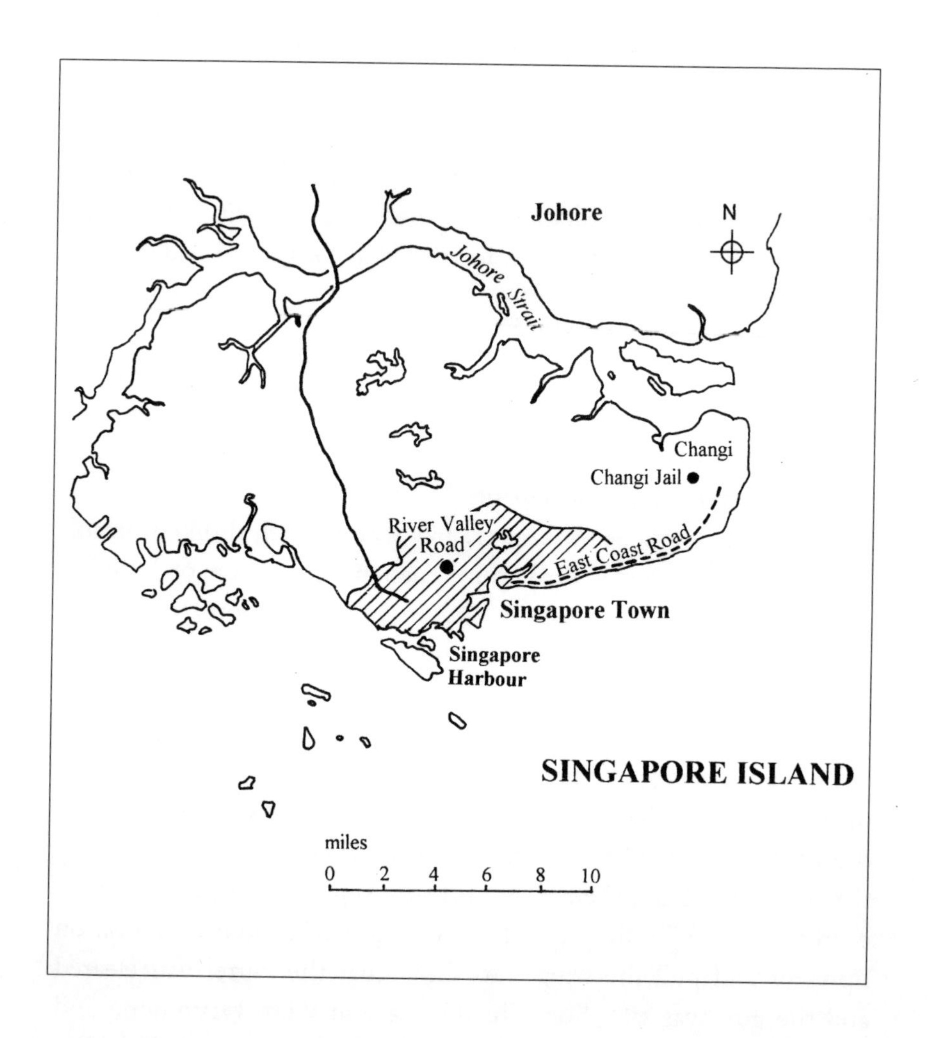
Johore
N
Johore Strait
Changi
Changi Jail
River Valley Road
East Coast Road
Singapore Town
Singapore Harbour
SINGAPORE ISLAND
miles
0 2 4 6 8 10

His belligerence flustered them more. Private Lionel Newman had struggled to remove his magazine and now the warrant officer was demanding to know if he had pulled the trigger to show the gun was unloaded. Newman overlooked the fact that he had not removed the round from the breech, pulled the trigger and the bullet whistled past the warrant officer's face. The man fled in the direction of the officers grouped several yards away screaming, 'Sir, Sir, they're trying to shoot me.' In any other circumstance the platoon members would have been delighted by the incident, but the occasion was not suitable for merriment. The platoon had given a good account of itself and possibly each and every soldier would have performed his duty fully, obeying orders manfully whatever the personal cost. But now it was over.

Ian Mitchell, who had enlisted a fortnight earlier, just five days after his seventeenth birthday, heaved a sigh of relief. It should have been clear to all that the alternative to surrender was annihilation of the Allied forces on the island within a day or so. It was therefore difficult to believe the sincerity of the one or two of his comrades who deplored the surrender. 'I would rather have fought to the bitter end than become a prisoner of war' was a protest Ian could not believe, particularly when made by intelligent people who surely had been able to read the writing on the wall.

That evening Captain Holiday told the platoon members that it had been easy to anticipate the surrender; he had therefore hidden away a suitable boat in which he had planned to take the platoon across the Johore Straits and into Malaya when the island surrendered. The intention would have been to make their way through Malaya, into Thailand and Burma, to join up with the Allied forces there. But senior officers had that evening vetoed his plan because it contravened the terms of surrender. He said he was proud of the platoon and that all had done their duty courageously. He regretted that Mervyn Kohloff had been killed and Dickie Hartley was missing.

The platoon slept well that night. That was not surprising because there had been no sleep for the previous three days and nights. The tensions were over and the din of battle had ended. Now they could rest and await the instructions of the Imperial Japanese Army.

The first news early next morning was that the unpleasant warrant officer had deserted. He had donned civilian clothes and disappeared after telling Sergeant Goodall his intention. He had written a cringing and apologetic note for the sergeant to read to the platoon members.

The men were also told that the Chinese and Malay companies of the Straits Settlements Volunteer Force had been disbanded to allow those men to return to their families, because it had been feared the Japanese would massacre them.

Ian heard that two Japanese soldiers were at the cross-roads nearby, looking just like cartoon caricatures of Japanese soldiers. Foolishly, he decided to have a look at them. But they saw him first and, shouting, they beckoned him over. He did his best to appear as though he was ambling over in an unconcerned way, but such nonchalance was difficult in the presence of two ferocious looking warriors. Certainly they wore those funny little caps, but not glasses; and they did not have large teeth and were not bandy-legged. They were wielding sub-machine guns, wore patchy beards and were shouting orders to any person who approached the cross-roads. They were nothing like the cartoon caricatures Ian had in mind. Orders were confidently shouted in Malay and English, parrot fashion, and disobedience, or even a failure to understand, was rewarded with a burst from the sub-machine gun; a Chinese man lay, probably dead, entangled with the cycle he had been riding. That they were fearsome warriors was certain.

And it was just as apparent that they were highly competent soldiers for whom it would be prudent to have, and show, respect and obedience. For a fleeting moment Ian reflected on the images he had held of Japanese soldiers, images which had made it so easy for him to believe that even an untrained youthful recruit like himself would be an adequate match for a Japanese soldier.

He had gone out equipped with a packet of cigarettes and a lighter, just in case; now he knew that that had been a good idea, and he produced them. The one who was obviously in command simply pocketed the packet and the lighter and Ian wisely did not express surprise. The warrior, pointing at Ian, demanded 'England *kar*? Australia *kar*?' Ian had a problem; he wondered who the Japanese hated more. Perhaps the wrong answer might mean immediate execution. He had an idea. 'I Singapore soldier,' he said. The Japanese became impatient and continued to demand, 'England *kar*? Australia *kar*?' Ian did his best to appear an idiot and persisted with his reply that he was a 'Singapore soldier'.

The Japanese expressed annoyance and changed the subject. 'How many soldiers in Singapore?' he demanded.

Ian tried to suggest by hand and facial expressions that he did not know. But the Japanese was getting angry.

'Forty thousand,' said Ian, scribbling that number on the dusty road.

Now the Japanese was more angry; he shouted and wrote '100,000'. Ian did his best to express agreement and surprise, whilst wondering frantically which of those two emotions was more imperative. Thankfully, the platoon sergeant, Frank Goodall, came to the rescue. Saluting the Japanese soldiers and gesticulating, he asked if the man could go back with him. The Japanese said, 'OK,' and was probably quite relieved to be rescued from such a half-wit!

The sergeant and Ian returned to the verandah of the house the platoon was occupying. Minutes later a Japanese soldier, accompanied by an Indian in his mid-twenties, arrived; the Japanese had come to take command of the pile of weapons. The Indian, who spoke fluent English and Japanese, was obviously the interpreter. Well dressed in western style, he seemed typical of the young Indian men who had worked as shop assistants in the Japanese ten-cent stores in Singapore's North Bridge Road prior to the outbreak of hostilities. It was very evident that he was a fifth columnist, but most of those present were prudent enough to keep their thoughts silent. But not Lancelot Sullivan. He was angered enough to challenge the Indian.

'How is it you speak Japanese?'

The Indian replied, somewhat passively, that he was Japanese. Sullivan was scornful. The Indian spoke to the Japanese soldier who fixed his bayonet and growled threateningly. All present were relieved that Sullivan had got the message and had shut up; they also now knew more about the sort of fifth columnists the Japanese had recruited and trained. They had a glimpse of what had been going on in those ten-cent stores, which had seemed to prosper despite a scarcity of custom.

That evening orders were received requiring all POWs to proceed to the Changi area the next day, Tuesday 17 February; they had to be beyond a specified line by 6 p.m.

Changi, the designated camp for POWs, was in the north-east corner of Singapore island. It contained groups of former British army barracks, residences for officers and married servicemen, and associated buildings, even well built coolie quarters. There were extensive grounds and playing fields. The area was bordered to the north by the sea, overlooking the Johore Straits and also the South China Sea. The site covered many acres, all parts of it being served by good roads. Before the outbreak of hostilities it had been a splendid place for soldiers to be stationed. Their only complaint then had been that the location was remote from Singapore town, where all the social action was!

In the recent past Ian had been there with his school cricket and rugger teams, to play against army teams. He had also visited friends, an army family, at their residence there, a fine detached house. He knew it could be a pleasant site for a POW camp, despite likely overcrowding.

They began their march to Changi early in the morning to avoid as much of the mid-day sun as possible. It was Ron Mitchell's eighteenth birthday. They were trying not to be downhearted; Norman Jackson played his harmonica and most were singing patriotic songs. Japanese soldiers by the wayside looked on in disbelief; many of them laughed at the Brits who were unashamed of their defeat. But it was too much for a passing Japanese officer who stopped his car and remonstrated with the platoon's officers. The men were ordered to stop singing and to march with humility commensurate with their situation. So they stopped singing, Jackson stopped playing his harmonica and they did their best to march with chests out and chins up, and in step. By now the roads leading to Changi were clogged with tens of thousands of POWs. And along the streets the Chinese civilian population looked on in silence and disbelief.

Some time before the 6 p.m. deadline the platoon reached the designated area where they could safely rest for the night. They moved away from the road and entered the large grounds of a house high above the East Coast Road. Barely had they settled when an angry Indian in his thirties strode up to them. 'Get off my land,' he ordered. 'You are British soldiers who have been defeated. You do not any longer have any rights to intrude.' The officers told him they would be leaving at 6 a.m. the next morning and there was no point in arguing further. But the man stayed and sought to repeat again and again that they were defeated British and their time had ended. Sullivan, of course, told him to get lost or suffer the consequences. The man left.

Some in the platoon were expressing surprise and dismay at the two incidents involving Indians. Then two Indian coolies arrived. They could not speak English but the POWs were able to communicate with them in Malay and with signs. They wanted to know how many soldiers there were, and would the soldiers permit them to bring some food. The Indians, probably Tamils, returned within the hour with bread and coffee which the POWs consumed hungrily. They asked when the POWs would recommence their march. Told that they would leave at dawn, the Indians asked if the soldiers would honour them by accepting breakfast before they left.

Before daybreak the next morning the Indians arrived quietly with more bread and coffee. The men breakfasted thoughtfully and with gratitude for the amazing generosity, kindness and courage of those Indian coolies. Asked how long it would be before the Japanese would be defeated, the soldiers forecast six months.

The march to Changi restarted. The platoon members were inevitably in thoughtful mood and in reasonable spirits. An advance party of two from the platoon had driven into the designated POW camp area the previous day with an army truck loaded with tinned food. Their intent was also to seek out suitable accommodation for the platoon to remain together. They had done well. The tins of food had been unloaded and hidden in premises previously used by Indian coolie families, and those premises when cleaned out would be home for the platoon. One of that advance party waited by the road at the approach to Changi and met the platoon, to guide his comrades to their new home.

Upon arrival at those former coolie quarters the men set to work cleaning and tidying and capturing the odd chicken which still happened to be about. But for the water shortage, which affected the entire POW camp at Changi, they were relatively comfortable. Certainly they were considerably more comfortable and better fed than the mass of other POWs, but it could not last long, and most knew that. Inevitably it was soon decreed that the platoon members had more space than was their proper share. And their officers, quite rightly, felt obliged to surrender their hoard of tinned food to the camp quartermaster to be shared by all at Changi.

The platoon moved into a battery of sixteen shower-rooms, each about six and a half feet square. Wooden board beds were brought with them from the coolie quarters, and with two to each shower-room the POWs in the platoon were still comparatively comfortable. A cookhouse was built, including an oven in an earth embankment, and the platoon members were able to draw rations and prepare their own food; the platoon's officers built a shack for themselves just a few yards away. The men in the platoon had almost become one large family!

But life was not idyllic: rations were poor and very short, water was not on tap and, in effect, was rationed. There was anger and sadness whenever Japanese guards machine-gunned hapless Malay fishermen whose little boats mistakenly came into firing range. A party of POWs, including some from the platoon, had been required to bury some sixty Chinese youths who, bundled into batches of four, had been taken to a nearby beach and machine-gunned. A survivor, who wasn't hurt at all, swapped clothes with some POWs, was given an army slouch hat and, suitably disguised, was smuggled back with the returning burial party to become a POW. He told the burial party that whenever the Japanese saw a group of three or more young Chinese men they would seize them and take them away for execution. That was what had happened to him. A chaplain POW, Captain Parr, who just a few months earlier was vice-principal of St Andrew's School at which

Ian was a student, had attended the burial. He told Ian that he recognised one of the victims who was a Chinese boy whom they both knew as a pupil of the school.

The Imperial Japanese Army issued an order to all POWs informing them that any attempt to escape would be punished by execution. Any POW found outside the camp without a Japanese escort would be deemed to be an escapee. Also punishable by execution was any disregard of IJA orders, any violence to any Japanese soldier or any disrespect towards the Japanese nation. No one doubted that every word was meant. Three soldiers who had not marched into Changi but had hidden in a red-light district in Singapore town were executed when the IJA caught up with them.

POWs well understood the threat to their lives. Even in those early days of captivity it dawned on them that were the Allies to invade a Japanese held territory, the Imperial Japanese Army would kill their prisoners rather than let them regain freedom. It was all very worrying.

The Imperial Japanese Army ordered all POWs to line the roads of Changi so that their all-conquering General Yamashita could be paid due homage during his victory tour. Any POW discovered evading attendance would be executed; POWs would be required to salute the general, or bow if they were not wearing hats. On the appointed day every POW had a hat! General Yamashita sat in his open-topped touring car which was driven slowly through Changi. Japanese soldiers were spaced along the route and the POWs obediently saluted. Yamashita was a stocky figure, quite unimpressive in his untidy uniform, but he was victorious. His car had been preceded and followed by cars with a film crew in each.

POW life in Changi was dull in the extreme. Rations, almost entirely made up of rice of a very poor quality, were of inadequate nutritional value, and water was still not on tap. Since there was no access to news bulletins and radios were banned, nothing was heard of the outside world.

The presence of dysentery became worrying and was causing some deaths. Ian had stomach pains and when he saw that he was passing blood and mucus the realisation that he had dysentery came as quite a blow. He and Norman Jackson had noticed each other making laboured trips to the latrines and each conceded he had dysentery. Both rapidly lost weight and were much weakened. Belatedly they visited the medical clinic where bacillary dysentery was diagnosed. They were given some M&B 693 tablets which cured them quickly.

Roll-call was held by the platoon's officers twice daily. The Japanese were informed of the outcome of these roll-calls and it was clear that if an absence was not reported to the Japanese and an escapee was subsequently captured, then the POW officer who concealed the absence would also be executed. Total control of POWs and their complete subservience to their captors was obtained by the Imperial Japanese Army very cheaply. The IJA needed only to show how brutal and murderous they were.

After a roll-call one morning Captain Holiday told the platoon that their duty had now changed. Their war effort was now to do all that was necessary to survive. They should look after their health and take no undue risks with the enemy; escape attempts would be futile. The Allied forces were a long way away and they had neither compasses nor maps; they would have nowhere to go and could easily be identified as escaped POWs. There was a reward on their heads. If an escapee was sheltered or helped by a civilian family, then that family would also face execution when the escapee was recaptured. Their duty was to survive and to be as healthy as possible at the war's end, for the sake of their families. The message was timely because many were young and foolhardy;

it made sense, and a thoughtful platoon of POWs dispersed in silence.

There was a secret radio in Changi, possibly more than just one. News was received that the convoy of ships which departed from Singapore on 6 February had reached Bombay safely. The ships were named in the bulletin and included the Free French ship *Felix Roussel.* Ian's mother and his sister Jean had been evacuated on the *Felix Roussel* on 6 February. Others in the platoon also had womenfolk evacuated in that convoy, but the joy and relief of the platoon was subdued because all knew that Lionel Newman and his two brothers were anxious about the safety of their womenfolk who had been evacuated in a convoy a week later, on Friday 13 February, just two days before the surrender.

Alas, there was no radio news of that convoy, and anxiety persisted because theirs had been a desperately late departure. So late, that the Japanese Navy would probably by then have infested the seas south of Singapore.

Indeed the evacuation attempt had been disastrous. Lionel Newman, and his brothers Ivan and Gordon, were later to learn that their mother, father and sister had perished when their ship was sunk by the Japanese Navy. Their younger brother Dickie had clung to wreckage to be washed ashore on a little island – later to be rounded-up and interned on the island of Riau.

The IJA regularly called for POWs to form working parties to be taken into Singapore town to undertake some task or other. But the platoon had not been called upon to supply men for any working party since the burial party at the beach at Changi, until Ian was told that he was required to join a party to work in town the next day. He looked forward to it. The platoon's officers furnished him with some money to buy food for the platoon if opportunity arose, but it was stressed that no undue risks should be taken and that the main priority was to return intact! The men were driven to the Singapore racecourse to clear up some war damage and debris. They were in an open lorry, standing. It was several miles to the racecourse and all thirty in the party had a hair-raising ride. They clung desperately to each other forming a swaying mass as the lorry sped unsteadily along the roads. There was not much other traffic about but the men did not have much opportunity to admire the outside world, their only preoccupation being to ensure they remained aboard that mad lorry! The Japanese driver probably thought he'd had an exhilarating drive.

At the racecourse they were formed into little groups. The work was not heavy but it was not enjoyable or uplifting either. At midday they were allowed to stop to eat the cooked rice they had brought with them. Ian wandered off with a few others, soon to be followed by most of the party. This relieved him quite a bit; safety in numbers was something he learned when he was a child! They headed for a street hawker selling bread at the entrance to the racecourse and he bought all he could carry, stuffing the rolls into his shirt. Others also made their purchases. Then suddenly two POWs burst through, pushed the hawker over, and stole some loaves. Most of the men were angered and collected amongst themselves to pay the Indian hawker for the stolen bread. He was grateful, but it was also evident that he was dismayed by what had happened. It seemed as though he was saying, 'Life is difficult enough in Singapore now. I never expected British people to behave that way.' Ian, and probably everyone else, felt very ashamed.

The guard in charge of the POWs during their lunch break had returned and found that the POWs had strayed, and were now returning. Almost all were concealing bread upon their person, but the guard did not realise it. He lined them up in two lines facing each other and proceeded to slap each across the face, scolding them at the same time. Fortunately everyone accepted the punishment without displaying anger or dissent. Donald Hare, a former public schoolboy with impeccable manners who was a model of good behaviour, decency and outlook, turned a bright shade of pink with embarrassment at the humiliation of it all.

The bread was hidden away for the afternoon whilst the men continued with their work, but each kept his eye on his precious purchase until work was over and it was time to be driven back to Changi. The return hair-raising drive did not differ at all, in the terror scale, from the outgoing journey. But all things considered Ian thought the excursion worthwhile, and this was especially so when he proudly produced his trophies which had been inside his sweaty shirt. Bread, even if crushed and sweat soiled, was still bread. And this was particularly so when compared with hibiscus leaves or snails which were now the extras of POW diet.

Ian's elder brother, Malcolm, had been admitted to the hospital at Roberts barracks, with enteritis. Visits to the hospital precincts in Changi entailed passing through an area of 'no-man's land'. POWs visiting the hospital had to be organised into parties and were required to carry an unfurled Japanese flag. They had to pass a guardroom manned by soldiers of the Indian National Army. These soldiers, still in uniform, wearing emblems of rank and still armed with British rifles, were formerly soldiers of the British led Indian Army who, just a few days after Singapore's surrender, had defected to the Japanese. Though not commonly realised by the POWs at Changi, only a fraction of the Indian Army had defected. British POWs passing through this 'no-man's land' were required to halt in front of the INA guardroom and salute, or bow if they were not wearing hats, before they could proceed further. And this had to be repeated on the return trip. It was usual for the INA soldiers to laugh, jeer and sometimes mockingly aim their rifles at the POWs, whose feelings about those in the INA were unfriendly.

Ian had the opportunity to visit Malcolm once before he, his brother Ron and others in the platoon were drafted into a 1500 strong workforce destined for a working camp of POWs in River Valley Road in Singapore town. It was about ten weeks since the surrender and all in the draft seemed pleased at the prospect of leaving Changi, though there was also some apprehension. It was said that more and better food would be supplied to working camps and, almost as importantly, water would be on tap and there would also be electricity. But the downside was that in Changi POWs rarely encountered their captors, whilst working sites would be littered with them. On the appointed day farewells were said. Those leaving Changi and those remaining behind wondered who would be destined to fare better.

Escorted by Japanese guards and loaded with their worldly possessions, which easily fitted into their kit bags, the fifteen hundred POWs left Changi camp on foot and were faced with a longish march. Just a few miles after leaving their camp in Changi they approached Changi Jail where the British, European and Australian civilians, including Ian's father, were interned; others in the party also had next of kin there. The march slowed and POWs waved and sang loudly, but they could not see any internees nor know whether they could be seen by them. But they hoped that, at the very least, some of the internees would have heard them and be cheered by knowing the morale of POWs was still high. And in that case, news of the event would surely spread through the jail like a bush fire. The singing of 'Rule Britannia', 'Sons of the Sea' and 'Land of Hope and Glory' could seldom have been better intentioned, nor ever shouted more loudly.

The march continued. The guards had been unhappy about what even they realised was more than just a sudden impulse to break into song, but the POWs had been careful only to slow their march rather than come to a stop, and the guards tolerated that even though with some impatience. It was, of course, a help that no Japanese officer was present or passing, because such a presence would certainly have spurred the guards into unpleasant activity.

A few miles further on the marchers reached areas where civilians, mostly Chinese, appeared and watched the POWs go by. They watched in silence. They were the older Chinese men and women and very young children. Probably no POW missed the significance that there were no young men or young women in that watching throng. The spirit of the march changed. It seemed the POWs sensed it would be improper to show good cheer in the presence of the Chinese population whom Britain had been unable to protect from their cruel enemy. The best that could be done was to meet the gaze of these people and try to convey a sympathetic and friendly smile. The POWs knew these people were suffering far greater hardships and fear of their oppressors than any of them had encountered in Changi. The presence of those civilians was probably felt by many POWs to be the only way those unfortunate and brave people could demonstrate their sympathy.

As the march advanced into more densely populated areas so the numbers of onlookers grew. The mood of the marchers, and of the onlookers, continued as before. But the edginess of their guards was much increased as evidenced by their heightened shouting and incessant nudging of POWs with rifle butts. Perhaps they were concerned that the destination would not be reached before dusk. More than likely they also feared the march might be behind schedule and that their superiors would punish them, because that was how the Japanese mind seemed to work. The tempo of the march increased and before dusk the River Valley Road camp was reached. All were glad to be at the destination at last.

CHAPTER 2

River Valley Road Camp

RIVER VALLEY ROAD was in the town area of Singapore, if only just. The POW camp, fronting onto and overlooking the road, comprised crude wooden huts built before the surrender to house bombed out families from any of Singapore's heavily populated areas. Each hut was about one hundred feet long and roofed with atap, a palm-leaf thatch. The huts had a central corridor from end to end, and the corridor ends were open. The floor was earth and on each side of the corridor were two wooden platforms, one above the other. The lower platform was about eighteen inches above the ground and the upper platform was about four and a half feet higher. The structure of each hut was such that the platforms divided naturally into bays, each bay having a frontage of about ten feet and a depth of about six and a half feet. The slope of the roof restricted headroom at the rear end of the upper platform. The upper platform of each bay was accessed by a ladder from the central corridor. The huts had electric lights, but insufficient to read by and there were pockets of darkness.

A dozen or more such huts, and other sheds for cookhouses and other facilities, made up the living areas of the camp. The site had piped water; latrines and showering areas were screened off, which was convenient because they were only just inside the barbed wire barrier and in sight of the road just thirty feet away.

In all there were about fifteen hundred POWs in the camp, and of these perhaps three hundred were Australian. The POWs were grouped within their units, their own officers being responsible for domestic arrangements, discipline and administration, but these were subject to overall Japanese control.

Each of the bays in the huts accommodated eight POWs, four up and four down. Upon arrival in the camp, Ian and Ron, with Charles Peel and Lionel Newman, all from the same platoon, grabbed an upstairs bay. Charles, probably in his forties and at least twice the age of the other three, would be a steadying influence. He was somewhat dour, had a strong moral code, always spoke his mind and strongly deplored the growing general tendency of POWs to use strong and obscene language at every turn. And, quite importantly, he had a presence strong enough to deter any young man from expanding his vocabulary – he would be good for the three young men!

The morning after arriving in the camp the POWs were paraded for roll-call, which was taken by Japanese guards. The men were in for more than one surprise. They were required to number-off in Japanese and had to learn to respond to commands in Japanese: 'forward march', 'right turn', 'left turn', 'about turn' and 'halt'. Then they were taught the IJA method of turning left, right or about. Initially there was a tendency for the POWs to laugh at all the cock-ups they made whilst being taught these skills. But the guards threateningly persuaded them that learning was urgent and important and humour was not allowed.

Some five hours or so were spent on those instructions and it was made clear to all that in future the Japanese culture would be omnipotent, and anyone who erred would be treated with brutality. The rest of the day was used by many to learn from each other how to number-off in Japanese. But it really was the case that the uneducated were teaching the uneducated and no one looked forward to the next roll-call which would be before dusk. It could be said, with pin-point accuracy, that confidence was not high.

At roll-call that evening, and thereafter to a progressively lessening extent, POWs lined up earlier than required, worked out their individual position in the line and then translated their English number to Japanese, as they understood it to be. Quite frequently a late arrival would walk down the line, count to the well rehearsed number which he thought he could pronounce with confidence, and then insert himself in that position. Every POW on his left, right down to the last of them, would have to advance the Japanese number he had been repeating to himself. Inevitably some would not have realised that their numerical position had been altered within the line, and would be in for a shock later. Matters were also not helped by the smart-arses who, quite legitimately, would use alternative Japanese words for certain numbers. For example, the number 4 would be pronounced *see* and 40 could be *see ju*. That would be the simple and accepted way of doing things. But an ultra-clever fellow would position himself at 40 to enable him to display his greater knowledge by saying *yon ju*, which was more correct. The unfortunate POW at 41 who had primed himself to say *see ju itchi* just as soon as he heard the fellow on the right say *see ju*, would be confused enough to fall apart if he heard *yon ju* instead. *Yon* instead of *see* could be used anywhere in the forties.

Laughter, or any kind of expressed amusement, during a roll-call generally led to face-slapping, and was not recommended. POWs soon learned that correct diction was not of ultimate importance. It was important to make some kind of loud multi-syllable sound urgently and confidently immediately after hearing the fellow on one's right shout his syllables. The Japanese guard, unable to make any sense of the accents and speed of it all, would follow behind the shouted sounds as he walked the line of POWs, wagging his finger at each, counting them for himself. It should have been hilarious, but it was not because hilarity would have given the game away, and in any case was not permitted. But there were always opportunities to have endless fun about it later when the guards were not about.

The Australians had the best roll-calls. The speedily shouted flow of foul and obscene words, intermingled with invective and insults to the IJA and all things Japanese, was almost incredible. Only the Aussies would try that on and, perhaps, only the Aussies had such a wonderfully suitable vocabulary which they adapted so well. Probably they had not bothered to learn even a single Japanese word. Why should they? Their own vocabulary, aided by their whine, could cope so well!

Each morning following roll-call the POWs were marched out of camp to work. Less than a mile away was some marshy land upon which they had to build some warehouses, but that would only be after the marsh was filled in. Half a mile away there was a hill which the men had to dig out and move to fill the lowland site. They worked in pairs, each pair equipped with two spades and a wooden cart of the kind which the IJA used in their campaigns to transport their equipment across roads or rough tracks. The carts had large wooden wheels and shafts. The work was heavy and the sun, fiercest between 11 a.m. and 3.30 p.m., made things considerably worse. The one hundred or so men engaged in this operation had a heavy task indeed; the track, between the hill they were digging into to fill their carts and the site at which they emptied them, was about half a mile long and littered with potholes, living roots of trees above ground and much rubble. At several points it was necessary for all but the biggest and heaviest pairs to manhandle the wheels of the carts to overcome obstructions. Ian and his brother Ron were paired, pulling and emptying their carts then returning for the next load. This tedious and exhausting work seemed endless. The presence of guards along the route ensured there was no slacking; the task would commence at 8 a.m. and continue until 5 p.m. with a half-hour break for lunch. In between, at two-hour intervals or thereabouts, there was a brief rest period. The guards would yell, *'Yas-u-mae,'* and all would savour their ten-minute respite from virtual slavery, which was now their lot on each working day.

The Japanese, in their own special way adept at maximising output, introduced a fixed task system. The task for each pair was set at thirteen loads per day. Each pair was issued with a piece of paper which had to be signed by the guard at the commencement of each journey – and he would not sign it if the cart was not adequately filled – and signed also by the guard at the dumping end. Twenty-six signatures were required before a pair could stop work. The IJA economised on their own manpower, too, because they no longer saw a need to maintain the few guards on the track between filling and emptying.

Ron and Ian, young and lightweight, were having a torrid time. Put simply, they did not have the physical stature to achieve the quota. But they were POWs in every sense and, like most others, were capable of getting around difficulties. And that was what they did!

Their scam was simple: they filled their cart in the normal way, got the signature of the guard and moved off down the track. Some hundred yards on they emptied their cart on some wasteland and dragged their empty cart to near the designated dumping site for that day. There, out of sight of the guard at the dumping end, they would partly fill their cart with earth which had been dumped there some days earlier. Then they would proceed to the designated area where they would tip out their light load. The IJA had not arranged any check to ensure that carts were indeed filled properly before being emptied at the dumping end. They had assumed that the one check at the filling end was adequate.

Ron and Ian were careful not to be too quick with their trips and rested and spent as much time as they thought necessary out of sight of the guards. They took pains not to give their game away to others who might copy them and ultimately bring their pretty little scheme to an untimely, and perhaps painful, end. So long as they were very careful they would no longer have difficulty getting those twenty-six signatures each day.

And so the work continued, day after each tedious day, with Ron and Ian still doing their negative work and remaining careful not to be found out. They were getting away with a lot but, if found out by their captors, they knew they could be in serious trouble. On one occasion it seemed the game was up, that they were found out and in fearful trouble. The guard at the dumping end was looking out for the arrival of the pair and spotted them just as they were coming round the corner after their usual improper re-loading. He yelled out to them, pointing and gesticulating to a heap of rocks nearby. The yelling was loud, urgent and persistent. Ron and Ian had seen a form of punishment imposed by the IJA in which the victim would be made to hold a rock, car wheel or any other heavy object in outstretched hands above his head in the blazing sun until the victim collapsed, and the heavy object would crash down on his head.

The pair thought the guard had discovered their scheme and was now intent on punishing them in the very special way the IJA seemed to enjoy. Ron and Ian pretended to be stupidly obtuse and would not go anywhere near the rocks at which the guard was pointing whilst gesticulating and shouting impatiently. The guard gave up and with evident frustration went to the pile of rocks from which he retrieved a tin of canned pineapple. He beckoned the pair over to him and handed over the tin, indicating that it was a reward for 'English soldier number one. Every day, first come first go.' It was probable that the guard had hidden the tin to avoid the risk that one of his superiors might discover it and take exception to the idea of having to bribe POWs to get work done.

The brothers accepted the bribe smilingly and with relief which they had to conceal. They knew then that their timing had become careless and it was important to slow down by having longer rests. They were also keenly aware that were that guard ever to find them out, his fury at having been made a monkey of would have awful consequences. They were tempted to end their game, but settled for the in-between. Thereafter they cheated on only one-third of their loads and reckoned that with continued care they would be safe. And so they were.

In due course the site had been filled in and the main construction job commenced. The POWs were divided into numerous little groups, each led by a NCO or warrant officer, and were used for the wide ranging tasks which warehouse construction would inevitably entail. Unloading, fetching and carrying, mixing concrete, laying foundations, sawing timber, erecting structures and so on, the POWs laboured whilst the guards supervised and organised. The control of operations by the Japanese was an eye-opener; they knew what they were doing. The work was lighter than previously when filling the site, and relations between guards and POWs were satisfactory. Few, if any, thought they had cause for complaint, even though the working day was long and the sun hot.

Like quite a few others, Ian had grown a beard. It was quite a good one, much fuller and thicker than the average seventeen-year-old could hope for. Indeed, it was more impressive than the beard grown by many of his elders. The alternative to growing a beard was to scrape one's face every second or third day with a razor blade, sharpened, and resharpened regularly on the inside curve of a glass or broken bottle. Growing a beard was easier! A guard, a quiet, unobtrusive and cheerful fellow, had admired Ian's beard. It was during a *yas-u-mae*, and he was trying to converse with the group of POWs in the hybrid language which had evolved. In this language, it often seemed that a guard would understand the English word if an 'o' was added to its end. Thus 'cigarette-o' or 'speedo' were easily understood if spoken by either captor or prisoner. Additionally, words could be joined together and the meaning would be understood providing this double word ended in the compulsory 'o'. For example, 'No-comprehend-o' was easily understood as meaning, 'I don't understand a word you are saying.'

But back to Ian's beard. Admiration of it was expressed by the guard, but when told that Ian was seventeen, he was at first disbelieving. He looked closely into Ian's face, then tugged the beard exclaiming joyously: 'You *ju-sitchi*. You baby soldier.' Ian playfully responded by indicating with his hand that he was quite a bit taller than the guard: 'I so high. You so high,' he said, then, pointing to the guard, added, 'You baby soldier.'

The guard became cross and scolded Ian at length. He was trying to indicate that he was a kind person, and had Ian made the remark to almost any other guard he would be killed. He did not threaten nor use any violence, and gradually all present realised the message he was conveying. The guard had been ridiculed when he was only being friendly and all present now understood how humiliating that was to him. Ian apologised to the guard who seemed to accept the apology and understood that he had not intended any disrespect, and was merely being playful. The incident was starkly etched in the young soldier's mind, and was an experience which would ensure he avoided similar dangers in the future.

Just a day or so later, whilst returning to camp after work, the men saw a Japanese officer playing with his pet baby monkey in the front garden of the house he occupied. The monkey was on the end of a chain which he held. Then, for no reason other than that the monkey had possibly disobeyed him, he swung the little creature on the end of the chain and crashed it to the ground. He then kicked the crippled animal and strode off.

The POWs were brought to earth starkly by what they had witnessed. Such unconcealed barbarism by an officer in the Imperial Japanese Army, against a defenceless and harmless baby monkey, his pet with which he had been playing seconds earlier, was sickening to behold. It was also frightening. None of the men could have missed the implications of being prisoners of an army officered by such as he. They were prisoners of unashamedly barbaric people, merciless bullies, spiteful and evil in their arrogance, even to the point that they were unconcerned that their barbarism was on display to be witnessed by any passer-by. Ian shuddered.

The Japanese administration had decreed that Thursdays would be rest days. Or as they put it, 'Thursday is all day Sunday, all time.' The men were paid ten cents per working day but had no means of spending their money. There were no shops or canteens in camp and talking to or dealing with civilians outside camp was prohibited. So money, even if it was only paper 'banana money', was accumulating, and in such circumstances black markets inevitably developed and flourished. Sure enough it gradually became possible for POWs to purchase items of food within the camp. Teams of Aussies started the black market and soon some Brits were at it too. The Aussies kept their cards close to their chests and their methods of operation remained a mystery. But a bold and enterprising handful of men in Ian's hut were doing it the big way. Certain Japanese sentries were bribed to arrange for civilian traders to pass baskets full of tinned food and cigarettes over the wire after dark. Just how these enterprising POWs were able to get the operations under way at the outset was a mystery which remained unsolved both by the curious and by those who wanted to get in on the act. The goods were sold from the black-marketeers' base in their hut for about 10% profit. The operators were no longer eating much rice.

Some POWs would take a chance. They would sneak away from their working party, make purchases from civilian hawkers and then return to work with a tin of something concealed on their person. But these were not black-marketeers since they could hardly bring in enough even for their own consumption.

Ian was keen to become an entrepreneur and learned that bare-faced cheek would often fool the guards; some POWs making purchases whilst on a working party had started bringing small crates of goodies back to camp. They had discovered that the guards would be fooled by brazenness. If a concealed item was found on a POW entering camp the guard would realise that it was an attempt at illicit smuggling. But a crate carried brazenly would get past the guard who would assume that since it was so overt it must be OK.

Ian proposed an import system to his brother. Ron thought it crazy, would have no part of it and strongly advised him against the idea. But Ian then put the scheme to his friend Lionel, who agreed it would probably work and that they should try it. They were poised to become black-marketeers. The plan was simple. On the next *yas-u-mae* day, Thursday, they would get hold of a wheelbarrow and a shovel and march boldly up to the camp gate, the one which opened onto waste ground which in days gone by had been used as a car park. The gate was chosen because a Chinese market-place was known to be nearby, beyond the waste ground. The hope and expectation was that the guard, if saluted with confidence, would assume their apparent request to be let out was authorised and that they were probably a part of a sanitary team. They would shop, and with their purchase concealed in the wheelbarrow, could then return to camp.

So on the next Thursday the two young soldiers got hold of

their wheelbarrow and shovel and marched, in step and in a confident manner, to the chosen gate. When they were just a few yards from the sentry at the gate they could see that the waste ground outside was being partly used by a company of Japanese soldiers who were being drilled by an officer. Not only had the sentry seen them and realised that they wanted to get out, so too had the Japanese officer. The two POWs, instantly and together, made the decision to go through with their bluff.

The POWs hadn't had time to think about it, but the fooling of the sentry was probably helped by the fact that the presence of the parading Japanese soldiers had not deterred them. The couple came to a full stop when Lionel shouted 'Halt.' They leaned the shovel against the wheelbarrow and saluted the sentry crisply. The sentry made a nodded bow, opened the gate, and the pair, with their wheelbarrow and shovel, were now outside the camp. They marched in step and as they neared the Japanese parade Lionel again shouted 'Halt.' They put down their wheelbarrow and shovel again, and saluted the Japanese officer with the smartest salute they could muster. The officer nodded acknowledgement, and Lionel and Ian indicated they wished permission to proceed around the outskirts of the parade. The officer, matching the politeness of the two British soldiers, parted his parade through the middle and waved the Brits through the opening. For that he received another very smart salute.

The two POWs proceeded to the market and decided against having a feast in a coffee shop. They had more than enough sense than to push their luck and were anxious to make their purchases and get back to camp quickly. Their purchases, mostly tins of corned beef, pilchards and the like, supplemented with some eggs, were placed carefully in the wheelbarrow, more than half filling it. A Chinese woman took them to a large dump of sand where they topped up the wheelbarrow and returned to the waste ground and the camp gate. The Japanese parade was no longer there. A halt, followed by a smart salute, gained them a nodded bow and entry into the camp.

They were relieved that all had gone well and complimented each other on their perfect reactions to the unforeseen events. That the Japanese officer had been so impressed with their bearing as to try to go one better by parting the parade, was an incident they knew they would cherish for all time. Now they, with Ron and Charles Peel, could enjoy the luxury of some tinned food and eggs, though all knew that many of the goodies would have to be sold for a 10% profit to finance the next excursion in the following week. Charles ate reluctantly; he was strongly against the whole idea and made his views known. He said he would not want any of the food which might be brought in in that way in the future. He would not concede that the two young soldiers had done anything other than be exceedingly irresponsible.

Despite knowing of Charles's displeasure, Lionel and Ian continued with their excursions on subsequent Thursdays. On one occasion the kindly guard, the one whom Ian had called a baby soldier, was crossing the waste ground. He was horrified to realise what the two were up to, and indicated by placing one wrist over the other and then moving his flat hand across his throat that they risked execution. He was anxious for their safety and the expression on his face spoke volumes.

The two young soldiers understood the warning and, in fact, hardly needed to be warned of the risks they ran. But they unwisely continued their weekly expeditions, gambling on not being caught out – and hoping that if caught they would, at worst, be only beaten up. Possibly it was an understandable gamble because rations were so poor and unpleasant that the rewards for their risks seemed great.

In their hut was a middle aged man in the SSVF, a loner who

had been a business man and then a public service employee in Singapore. The man 'Z' had his pet dog, a black Scottie, with him in camp and he was more concerned about the welfare of his pet than that of any other man. Z had obviously taken care to bring with him a great deal of money when the POWs had first marched into their prison camp at Changi. He now purchased from POWs all the gold rings and other precious valuables, such as watches and fountain pens, that he could lay his hands on. Having acquired a goodly hoard, he set about arranging for cigarettes and food to be smuggled into the camp.

But Z was a shady person, a manipulator who never risked his own skin but instead paid others to smuggle in tins of food for himself and his dog, and also to sell for profit. Ian and Lionel both knew of Z's reputation and, in any event, disliked the man every bit as much as others disliked him. He had offered substantial profits in attempts to persuade them to bring in beer for himself, rather than to continue trading in tinned food. Z's men had, presumably, refused to bring in beer – naturally enough, perhaps, because of the seeming certainty that, if caught, punishment for bringing in alcohol would be severe indeed. The two young men were not persuaded, even though they knew that some men were trading in beer.

Neither were they impressed by Z's pleas to them to increase their profit margin because it was bad business to make only slight profits when greater profits were there for the taking. His justification was that they were taking serious risks, and merited greater rewards, but that was unconvincing because both the young men knew him to be the very last person to be concerned about the welfare of anybody else. Z was left with the problem of paying his men out of a very small profit margin. The amount of tinned food brought in by those two young soldiers was small, but even so, it seemed to them now that they helped to keep down prices in that camp. Initially their only objective had been to get for themselves some better food to eat. But it must also have been apparent that their weekly adventure added spice to their existence and, though modest for most of the time, they enjoyed the beefing up of their macho!

On each successive Thursday more pairs of POWs were emulating them. Lionel and Ian were now anxious and agreed the game would be played out before long. As they set out one Thursday they pledged that it would be their last outing. They had seen some ten pairs precede them and their good sense told them to stop immediately, but young men do not always follow their more sensible instincts. Perhaps because neither wanted to admit he had become scared, they proceeded with their shopping expedition. The sentry had let out all the preceding pairs, and now he opened the gate once more to let out these two. There was no problem so far.

The two young men did their shopping and then, having topped up with sand, started for home. As soon as the camp gate came in sight they saw trouble. Lined up outside were all the pairs who had already returned from their expedition. Their wheelbarrows were upturned and all tins of food bayoneted and eggs smashed. The pair approached the angry sentry who then upturned their wheelbarrow, bayoneted the tins and lined up the pair alongside the others.

They must have been the last pair because the sentry counted them and seemed satisfied. He went down the line, slapping the face of each man in turn; then he made each slap his partner's face. The sentry scolded them severely and told them that most other Japanese soldiers in his position would call in the Kempi-tai, the equivalent of the Gestapo. And he made it clear the only outcome of that would be execution. Ian wondered if his kindly guard had informed on them so that this sentry would warn the

POWs they were taking ridiculous risks. Lionel and Ian returned to their friends somewhat sheepishly. The lining up of the POWs had been seen by others in camp and had caused some anxiety. When they returned everyone laughed, probably with massive relief, at the POWs who thought they were entrepreneurs. As days went by Ian became more and more convinced that his friendly guard had informed on them, in a well intentioned and successful way.

Some days later another POW developed a plan for his own solo shopping sprees. It entailed a high risk, seemed insane and would need a miracle to work. The man, who was intelligent and scholarly, reputed to be a scientist of some kind, seemed a very unlikely person to think up or execute any escapade, and definitely not such a mad-cap one. He was a loner, but that did not matter because there could be no chance anyone would wish to join him in his outlandish plan. He had acquired some knowledge of Chinese characters and knew of their similarity with their Japanese counterparts. He made an armband and on it wrote, in Japanese characters, a permit for himself to wander freely. There were many people about with official Japanese armbands and he must have felt confident he would get away with it. And so he did, with style, too.

The sentry at the gate had let him out at about 9 a.m. that Thursday morning. He had walked many miles through many streets, had made purchases in markets and shops, had eaten in a Chinese coffee shop and even rested there before leaving to return to camp late in the afternoon. By then he had lost his bearings so he asked a Japanese warrant officer on a motor cycle combination for directions, and the Japanese soldier brought him back to camp in his side-car.

However, there was trouble in store for him. Before leaving in the morning he had leaked his plan, and would not be deterred despite dire warnings. He was watched as he successfully left camp and until he disappeared down the road. When he had not returned by the early afternoon his absence was reported to the officer in charge of his hut. Anxiety grew and the road was watched hopefully. At just before 5 p.m. the Japanese soldier on the motor cycle, with the POW in the side-car, were seen arriving at the camp gate. The POW thanked the Japanese soldier, and the sentry opened the gate to allow him in.

Unfortunately for the man he could not appreciate the worry he had caused, and neither apologised nor agreed never to do such a thing again. His attitude was foolish because, unless perhaps he could have proved to the Japanese that he was mad, he would have faced severe punishment had he been caught out. And if he had failed to be back in time for roll-call, which was only about half an hour after his return, then his absence would have had to be reported to the Japanese with terrible consequences for him. For if the absence had not been reported and he had been caught, then the officer who failed to report the roll-call absence would also face the prospect of punishment. In the circumstances it was difficult to feel sorry for the man when he was put on a charge and subsequently sentenced to cookhouse fatigues on evenings and Thursdays. He was also ordered never again to venture out. The man was indignant. He thought his treatment resulted from cowardice, and was vehement in his protestations that when the war ended he would lodge a formal complaint against the officer who had dealt with him.

So risky had the escapade been that there was little, if any, admiration for it, and no one thought he had been hard done by. Many did think that the action against him might deter him from further escapades, which might possibly save his life, and perhaps the lives of others too.

Towards the end of the period when Ian was undertaking those shopping expeditions he stopped presenting himself for work each day because his boots had worn away. Others had been doing that for some weeks, so it seemed a safe enough thing to do. It was quite simple, all he had to do was join the people authorised to stay in camp each day immediately after the morning roll-call. Those authorised were the camp cooks, sanitary workers, medical people and sick. Those remaining would march out to work.

It was a little worrying though, because the bootless grew in number each day. Ron thought Ian was again taking a foolish risk and advised him to abandon the lark. But staying away from manual work in the blazing sun was the tempting option that Ian had taken, and he would not readily abandon that life of ease.

Some weeks after he had joined them, Ian and his bootless comrades were in for a horrendous fright and some punishment. In the middle of the day a horde of Japanese rushed into the camp making much noise and showing much urgency. All personnel were required to parade; the cooks, sanitary people, medics and walking sick were then dismissed, leaving behind only the bootless.

They were all made to run out through the gate on River Valley Road and onto a grassed area facing the camp. There the one hundred or so men were lined up in three lines forming three sides of a square. Everything was hurried and there was much shouting; some twenty Japanese, with bayonets fixed, lined the road and faced the POWs. Then a Japanese army truck arrived and three machine-guns removed from it were set up facing the POWs, each gun attended by two soldiers. A Japanese staff car pulled to a halt and an officer came out purposefully, followed by another, each with a scroll in his hand. The POWs were ordered to salute the officers, and then the one who was obviously senior read his proclamation in Japanese.

He was angry, fierce and threatening, and the word *Bushido* occurred frequently. The POWs knew they were in very serious trouble; Ian, and probably everyone else, thought there was a more than even chance that they would soon be executed. And if any POW lost his head and panicked because of the terror of it all, he, and probably most others too, feared that the mowing down would be started even if it had not been intended in the first place. The proclamation was a long one and the longer it lasted the more it seemed that execution would follow.

Tears flowed from the eyes of many. Ian's tears were because he felt he'd let down his mother and sister and they would suffer much grief in due course. He recalled Captain Holiday's words about not taking undue risks with the enemy; he had taken so many risks despite the pleas of Ron, Charles Peel and others.

His head full of those thoughts, and his eyes brimful with tears, he suddenly realised that the other Japanese officer was now reading the proclamation in English. The gist of the proclamation was that the Japanese nation, because of their culture and generous spirit and in accordance with the spirit of Bushido, had spared the lives of the British soldiers when they were defeated. In line with this generous spirit the Japanese nation had offered the hand of friendship to the British soldiers who had thrown themselves at the feet of the Japanese and accepted defeat. As friends, the Japanese nation had offered the opportunity of working for the Divine Emperor so that the British soldiers could redeem themselves. Without a willingness to accept the chance of redemption there could be no hope for the British soldiers, and Bushido, which is the spirit of all that is fair and honourable in battle, was greatly offended. Today the British should be punished. But should the generosity of the Japanese nation be spurned again then those who offended the spirit of Bushido would be executed, because fairness in conflict was the way of the Japanese people.

Thus, it was not until late in the proclamation that the POWs learned they were not to be executed on this occasion. So much for Japanese generosity. The tears were soon quelled because their punishment was about to start. The POWs were made to run to the waste ground on the other side of the camp, the ground the shopping expeditions used to cross. There they were made to run around the perimeter, and were encouraged to do so speedily by Japanese soldiers with whips. The track had been generously sprinkled with broken rubble and as the POWs ran they tried to pick their way through to save their bare feet from as much punishment as possible. But the Japanese with whips did not approve of this attempt to partially evade punishment, and thus it was not only feet that were damaged before the punishment was ended after five laps. A smile came to the face of many when a POW asserted, 'I won't do a lap of honour, not even for that bugger Bushido.'

Whilst the POWs were being given the run around a British officer demanded that the event be stopped. His demands were refused, and might even have caused more laps to be run than planned. At best, his request had to be refused, and be seen to be refused, because a contingent of Chinese men, women and children had been forced to watch the humiliation of the British. And, no doubt, 'that bugger Bushido' had insisted upon the presence of the civilian population too.

Back in camp the bootless men were paraded before the officer, still in the blazing sun. He spent rather a long time talking and kept the weary men on their bare torn feet whilst he told them that he would lodge the strongest possible protest with the Camp Commandant, and would also do all in his power to get boots for them. Some POWs began muttering angrily, and the muttering spread far and wide at quite a pace. In mid-sentence the officer suddenly realised that he had got it all wrong and broke off to dismiss the parade.

At the end of the day when the working parties returned to camp there was much amusement at the expense of the bootless men. The workers had not been told of the mental torture they had endured and did not know of the full horror of that day. The victims could not readily tell of the horror of facing an execution squad, even if execution did not follow. A salutary lesson had, no doubt, been learned by the victims. None could have learned more thoroughly than Ian.

The bootless men all reported for work the next day; most were bare footed. Surprisingly their wounded feet healed quickly enough, but even so there was an urgency in their quest for footwear. The construction of the warehouse was proceeding rapidly, but this was to be expected considering the size of the work-force and the Japanese methods of inducing high output from the POWs. Some of the buildings were, in fact, nearing completion and IJA stores were being stacked within them. The POWs engaged in moving those stores and stacking them were somewhat frustrated – their opportunities to steal were frequent, but IJA caps, boots and uniforms would be of little use to them. Even for the bootless men there could be no point in acquiring undersized IJA boots which, at best, would provide great discomfort and untold risks. But, even so, men foraged persistently in the hope that something worthwhile would surface.

The intake of smuggled food and cigarettes into the camp continued apace. The big boys had well developed arrangements, mostly involving the bribing of guards and the delivery of large cases of tinned food after dark. The ability to purchase the occasional tin of food or egg in camp made life more interesting.

An indication of the cost of contraband food in the camp can be gauged from the following examples: corned beef was priced at seventy cents a tin, a large tin of pilchards was sixty cents, an egg was fifteen cents. The men were paid ten cents per working day, and since Thursday was not worked, their weekly income from work was a maximum of sixty cents. So those who could not supplement their pay could afford no more than about one tin of food a week to enhance a dull diet of low quality rice and a little unappetizing vegetable.

Others would trade any valuables they had, some inside camp with one of the big boys, some outside camp whilst at work, some with guards. One way or another the camp had become very active after dusk each day. Wares would be on display and would-be purchasers would look out for a good buy. Sometimes men would hawk around fresh fruit or exotic contraband like beer, and their cries of 'Ripe bananas' or 'Tiger beer' would ring out.

Once Ian bought a few pounds of peanuts whilst on a working party and he was back in business again, or so he thought. But he roasted them in a tin can over a wood fire in the dark – and he'd never before seen peanuts being roasted, not even in daylight – so he finished up with peanuts which were quite well burnt. He had invested all his savings in those nuts and was therefore undeterred. He hawked them in an Aussie hut, in semi-darkness. His 'Hot roasted peanuts, lovely and hot, freshly cooked, only ten cents a portion' were sold quickly. Then, wisely, he departed quickly and avoided the Aussies for a week or two.

And such incidents were part of the everyday events after dusk in River Valley Road camp. Life there was not boring in any way, and there was another activity, too. The Aussies had gambling tables and a seemingly insatiable appetite for gambling, especially on 'Two-Up' which involved tossing coins and forecasting how they would land. Activity around those tables was intense, and gambling there was enjoyed by some Brits too. Ian watched in disbelief as substantial stakes were wagered. But gambling, in any form, was not tolerated by the Japanese so the gambling promoters always posted their sentries at strategic points to warn of the approach of the enemy.

Another after-dusk activity was the concert party which was in full swing every evening in the 'theatre'. There, impromptu performers would sing, tell stories, recite verses, tell jokes or juggle according to their varied abilities. Every performer was cheered, even if he was only repeating his one and only masterpiece which had been heard on countless previous occasions. And the singing of patriotic songs by the entire audience seemed to lift everyone there. They sang as loudly as possible, believing that the Chinese civilian population would hear them and know that the British had obviously not lost hope.

Under the circumstances the camp was a lively place, far better than the boredom of Changi. The POWs preferred the camp to Changi despite the added risks, more face slapping, more threats and more beatings. Even the risks had an upside: they added excitement to what could otherwise be a humdrum existence. And, of course, there was more to eat.

Two lorries carrying Gurkha POWs passed the River Valley Road camp each evening. The Gurkha drivers would toot their horns and the British POWs lining the wire would exchange 'V' signs with them. The Japanese guards on the passenger seats of the lorries, and the sentries at the gates of the British camp, tolerated the quaint behaviour of the POWs. Since this exchange of greetings between the Gurkhas and the British had not been witnessed by any Japanese officer, it was allowed to continue. Then the Japanese sentries at the gates were replaced by soldiers of the Indian National Army.

The INA sentries were as unpleasant as they could possibly be, and sought to show the British POWs that they were in charge now. A smouldering resentment against the INA soldiers was inevitable, but at the same time the POWs were careful to avoid giving the INA sentries any opportunity to scold or hit or arrest. It had become paramount that the INA sentries be given little, if any, chance to assert themselves. But those sentries, seeing the daily exchange of greetings between the Gurkhas and the British, tried to put a stop to it by shouting and aiming their rifles at the British who were lining the wire awaiting the Gurkhas. The POWs ignored the INA sentries, pretending they weren't there. When the Gurkhas arrived their drivers slowed, as usual. They got the picture immediately. The lorries stopped quickly, their Gurkha occupants rushed towards the INA sentry at the gate, and the INA sentry fled into the camp for safety. The Gurkhas returned to their lorries where their Japanese guards could be seen laughing hilariously. The exchange of greetings between the two sets of POWs was prolonged, and then the Gurkhas drove off. The men in River Valley Road camp were elated, and no more notice was taken of the INA sentries in that camp.

On some days parties of POWs were marched to the docks to load or unload cargo vessels. Usually it was empty oil drums that the POWs had to manhandle or roll. If those drums had been standing in the sun and if it was already afternoon, then the men had a tough time. They were not equipped with gloves or any protection for their hands, so the drums, roughened with rust and heated by the sun, were a formidable problem. To make matters worse, the guards there were not the usual ones and obviously had not previously had charge of British POWs. Communications were difficult, and it always had been the case that misunderstanding between POWs and a new set of guards led to work problems, time wasted, frustration and ultimately bad temper by the guards, with all kinds of outcomes.

Even so, working at the docks was a change and did involve a half-hour march, which was not a bad thing since it reduced the length of the time POWs would spend on tedious and unpleasant work. Furthermore, the route was through streets in populated areas, and the sights and sounds added interest to POW life. Another good aspect was that on these marches the POWs would often sing and they were always lifted by the singing of 'Rule Britannia' or other patriotic songs. And if their captors had been particularly unpleasant, then the singing of the rude version of Colonel Bogey, as expressively as possible, was always satisfying. And the POWs always felt that the civilian population, too, would be lifted. However, one day a Japanese officer in a passing staff car stopped and ordered the singing to cease. He was extremely angry and the guard felt the lash of his tongue.

On one occasion Gurkha POWs were also at the docks. The guards kept them apart from the British as best they could but in any case dialogue between the two sets of POWs was difficult in the extreme. Only one Gurkha spoke any English at all, and his knowledge of the language was sparse. But the Brits were able to learn from him that the IJA were still trying to persuade Gurkhas to change sides, and had resorted to bribes and threats. A unit from the Indian National Army had been moved alongside the Gurkha camp and were attempting to encourage the Gurkhas to defect. Pressure was being exerted on individuals, and the Gurkhas as a whole were having a rough time. The conversation was brought to an end as soon as a Japanese guard noticed the get-together. The British wanted to know if they were the same Gurkhas who regularly drove past the River Valley Road camp, but they were not given a chance to find out. Thereafter, the exchanges of greetings between British and Gurkha POWs seemed to be ever more meaningful and worthy to the Brits.

Separated from River Valley Road camp by about two hundred yards, through the middle of which was a stream spanned by a wooden bridge, was Havelock Road camp which was a working camp with about a thousand POWs. Contact between the occupants of the two camps was not allowed, the IJA having turned down a request to permit a passage between the two camps on rest days. Guards occasionally patrolled the area between the camps, but the patrols were infrequent.

Graham, a POW in Ian's hut, was a man of some spirit and enterprise; he fairly regularly visited Havelock Road camp after dark because he had friends there. He did not use subterfuge to conceal any such trip, but had prepared a good act and story to help him out of trouble, if he was caught. And one bright moonlight night he was caught.

His soul mates, with whom he shared a bay in the hut, realised that something was wrong when he had not returned by very late at night. Everyone saw Graham the next morning; he was tied to a lamp-post in front of the IJA guardroom which was outside the camp and just across the road. His face was bruised. An anxious watch was kept on him and soon two Japanese arrived; they took him into the guardroom where he was kept for about half an hour. When he emerged he was smiling, and the Japanese sergeant had a pleasant enough expression on his face, too.

Graham was returned to the camp and related his story to his eager friends. He told them that whilst on his way back from the Havelock Road camp he realised that a patrol was in the vicinity and thought he would probably be caught, so he back-tracked to the wooden bridge he'd already crossed, and remained on it so that he would be easily seen. Whilst waiting to be seen he whispered loudly to himself and gazed upwards towards the moon.

The Japanese patrol had seized him and he had been taken back to the guardroom where he was tied to the lamp-post. Whenever the guard changed, which was every four hours, the new set of guards slapped him about the face. Some time after daybreak there was telephone activity in the guardroom and subsequently a sergeant and interpreter arrived to interrogate him. He simply explained to the sergeant that he was sorry he had caused all the fuss. He said he was a poetical person and had been carried away by the beauty of the bright night; he had not been able to resist the temptation to visit the bridge briefly, to see the moon reflected in the moving water of the stream below. Whilst standing there he was delayed from returning because he had a powerful urge to compose a poem there, with the moon above and the moving water below.

The sergeant had seemed amused. The interpreter asked Graham to recite the poem he had composed. Graham recited the verse involving brightness, water, sky and reflections which he had composed during the night whilst tied to the lamp-post. The interpreter was impressed; he and the sergeant exchanged words and smiles and Graham was told that he must not do it again, but they were sorry he had been injured and could return to his friends immediately. They gave him a packet of cigarettes to compensate for the injuries.

Graham's audience chuckled whilst he told his tale. But he would not recite his poem to them; he said he would not be able to live it down if they knew just how poor it was. And he challenged any of them to compose poetry whilst tied to a lamp-post all night, however bright the moonlight.

In mid-September 1942, some seven months after they had been taken prisoner, the POWs were provided with postcards for them each to send a message to their next of kin. They were required to write in block letters and were told that the longer the message, the longer it would take for the Japanese censors to deal with it.

Brief and simple messages were recommended if there was to be any chance at all for the cards to reach their destinations in time for Christmas. The men were glad of the opportunity to tell their families they were alive and were prisoners of war, because all of them believed it unlikely that the IJA had provided lists of names of prisoners to the Red Cross, as had been their civilised obligation. Many thought they should include all their forenames, nicknames or pet names, or include a personal message, or by some other means indicate to their folk that the cards had been written by themselves. They felt there might not be another opportunity to ease the minds of their families.

As the days and weeks slowly passed, many were the discussions about the likely length of the war. The men did not consider how long it would be before the Allies recaptured the territory in which they were held. Such thoughts would be morale sapping because of the seeming inevitability that the IJA would massacre their prisoners rather than let them regain freedom, and this was not something the men wished to have at the forefront of their minds. They knew that their survival and freedom could come about only if there was an end to the war which did not involve defeating the Japanese in battle, or siege, in the country in which the prisoners were themselves held. So the discussions concerned only how long it would take for Japan to sue for peace.

A small group of men in the Straits Settlements Volunteer Force, all of them intelligent and worldly in a business sense, were confident of their prediction that the war might last until the end of 1945. They were equally confident that it would not end before February 1945, some three years after the men had been taken prisoner. Their prediction, based on the acceptance of the strategic facts of the situation in Europe and in the Far East, as existed at the time of their capture, cheered hardly anyone. The sense and logic of their assessment gave considerable credence to their view, but the thought of another three years or so of captivity was something it was better not to think about.

Ian accepted the prediction as being a valid one, but the prospect of another three years in Japanese captivity was unpalatable to him. He knew he could face up to the prospect of another six months of being a POW with reasonable good cheer, so he told himself that the Japanese would throw in the towel within about six months, and that was all he wanted to know. Some of his elders sometimes bemoaned the fact that more than six months of their lives had been wasted in captivity. Ian kept his thoughts about that to himself, but wondered how intelligent people could not see that time already spent in captivity was not wasted but was part of a total span of time which had to elapse before the war could end. Therefore it was good, rather than bad, that at least that amount of time had already passed. And that simple and irrefutable logic boosted Ian's morale on every occasion that any of his older comrades depressed proceedings by moaning about the months already wasted. In the circumstances which prevailed, could anything be more important to any of them than that with each passing day, week, month or year they were that much closer to freedom for themselves, and for all others whom the Japanese had enslaved?

And, as for Ian's belief that the war would end within six months, well, he reviewed that view on the first of January and on the first of July regularly. And on each occasion he was cheered by the certain knowledge that he was more likely to be right than he had been six months earlier. In his mind, the passing of each six-month period was a milestone and a worthwhile event, deserving cheers rather than tears. And he never shed that philosophy.

Ian had successfully stolen a pair of canvas boots from the warehouse, but was cautious about wearing them. The problem was that they were so obviously Japanese army issue because there was a separate compartment for the big toe, this being a feature of their canvas boots which were designed for better foothold when climbing trees or moving across rough terrain. But he had thought about it and had prepared his story to explain their acquisition. And now that he wasn't working at the warehouse he wore the stolen boots rather than continue to be barefooted.

Sure enough he was challenged by a guard who clearly indicated that the boots were stolen. Ian deserved an Oscar for his performance of pained indignation. Shaking his head sadly he told the guard that a Japanese officer had very kindly given him the boots when he noticed that he was barefooted whilst marching to work. He did not exactly ask for an apology, but his deeply hurt look coupled with a continuously slowly shaking head, was enough for the guard to acknowledge he had made a terrible mistake.

But a few days later he discarded the boots because he had developed a nagging fear of the consequences of being found out. Images of the mock execution squad he had faced weeks earlier were haunting him more since he stole the boots, and being barefooted was a better alternative than a continuing risk of being found out, with all its likely consequences.

The Bishop of Singapore was allowed some freedom to pursue pastoral duties including visits to POWs in their camps, if on a Thursday, or at the larger work sites on working days. He did not seem to be escorted and was happy to carry innocent personal messages to and from POWs or internees in Changi Jail. Unknown to the Japanese many written messages, generally just greetings, were so transported, including one from Ron and Ian to their father in Changi Jail.

The IJA decreed that every POW had to sign a pledge that he would not attempt to escape. The pledge also acknowledged the right of the IJA to execute the POW if caught preparing or attempting to escape, or whenever caught after an escape. The senior British officer responded by informing the IJA that the British POWs were unable to give such an undertaking because they were all bound, by British Army Regulations, to escape if opportunity arose.

The IJA's response was to move, over a period of three days, thousands of POWs from Changi into Selarang Barracks, which was a barrack block whose precincts were surrounded by a concrete parade ground. There was a standpipe for water, but no sanitation facilities worthy of mention – in relation to the total of fifteen thousand POWs who were poured into the 15,000 square yards of their concentration camp. The IJA surrounded the camp with barbed wire and machine-gun posts.

By the third day the whole prison was so dense with POWs that some climbed into the rafters of the building whilst others were perched on lamp-posts. The men, with mugs in hand, were a continuous moving mass advancing past the only stand-pipe.

On the third day diphtheria was reported. Worse would follow if the Senior British Officer remained obstinate, because the IJA declared that the sick in the hospital at Changi would be moved into the concentration camp the next day. Medical officers advised that, even without the addition of the sick from the hospital at Changi, the situation was on the verge of being disastrous. The Senior British Officer then told the IJA Command that he would order the men to sign the document, saying that they would thus be exonerated from blame for breaching British Army regulations. The IJA kept the POWs in their concentration camp for a further twenty-four hours.

News of the atrocity, whilst still in progress, reached the River Valley Road camp. None had any doubt at any stage that the Japanese would not alter their minds, since to give way to prisoners for whom they had absolute contempt would be a 'loss of face', which would be intolerable to the IJA. It was difficult to understand why the senior British officer had not realised that in the first place, for if he had realised it, how could he possibly have failed to foresee that terrible consequences to his men would follow his defiance?

Dietary deficiencies were having their effect. A skin complaint, known as 'itchy balls', was making itself felt and there were more and more victims of this irksome complaint. The skin of the scrotum would dry, crack and flake off and the unfortunate man would have a maddening itch which he could not leave alone. But all the scratching in the world did not help the sufferer. Some tried rubbing salt into the raw skin, preferring to have pain rather than a maddening itch, but that achieved nothing other than to leave the sufferer with pain and an itch. Lionel Newman, and some others who were more badly affected than most, were sent back to Changi where it was hoped that proper medical attention and some vitamins would be available.

The medical officers advised all sufferers to avoid scratching because of the risk of introducing infection to the area, pointing out that were there to be an infection the end result could be a need to remove the victim's testicles. Before long almost everyone in the River Valley Road camp had 'itchy balls' and were all striving to develop the required level of will power to ensure that they did not lose them. Then, over a short period, the ailment disappeared as suddenly as it had arrived.

The men had been prisoners for some seven months and the stage was reached where underpants were a luxury few of them had. The Japanese soldiers did not have underpants, as such. Instead they wore a cloth about twenty-four inches long and seven inches wide, with a cord attached to one of the narrow ends. The cord would be tied around the waist and the hanging cloth taken under the crutch and brought up to the front to be tucked under the cord; the end of the cloth would then hang skirt like. Inevitably some POWs started to make these skimpy garments for themselves. Just as inevitably, they were asked by their friends if they had become 'Jap-Happy'. The skimpy garment was easily made and easily washed; it was effective, and under the circumstances ideal for prisoner of war life. More and more men were wearing them and they became known as 'jap-happies'. In due course they displaced shorts and trousers and became the only clothing most men had. The name 'jap-happy' became universal in all camps.

The Japanese let it be known that some tins of food and a few comforts had been received from the International Red Cross for distribution. At the same time they announced that the British POWs in camp were soon to be moved to Thailand, and suggested that the POWs should retain their Red Cross food for the journey. The share-out of food amounted to less than two tins per person and the cigarette allocation was only a little more generous. But there were enough trilby hats to go round. Not many saved their tinned food for the journey, it being too tempting to savour tasty food which had been inadequately available to most in recent months.

The cigarettes, made in India, were of a brand not previously known to them. They were 'VICTORY' brand, and there was a full sized 'V' on one side of the packet. Predictably enough every man cut out the 'V' and wedged it in the band of his trilby. Most were expecting the Japanese to order the removal of that symbol from the hats, but the Japanese could not have known about the 'V' symbol and there was no objection from them. There were still a few days of working at the docks before leaving for Thailand, and the POWs were happy to march through the streets with their 'V' symbols on display, until the appointed day.

It was the middle of October 1942, just eight months after their surrender, that the men left River Valley Road on foot bound for the railway station. The streets were lined by the local populace, mostly Chinese, who looked on in silence. The prisoners would have preferred not to leave River Valley Road camp which they had developed into the best camp they would ever be in, even if they did not know it at the time.

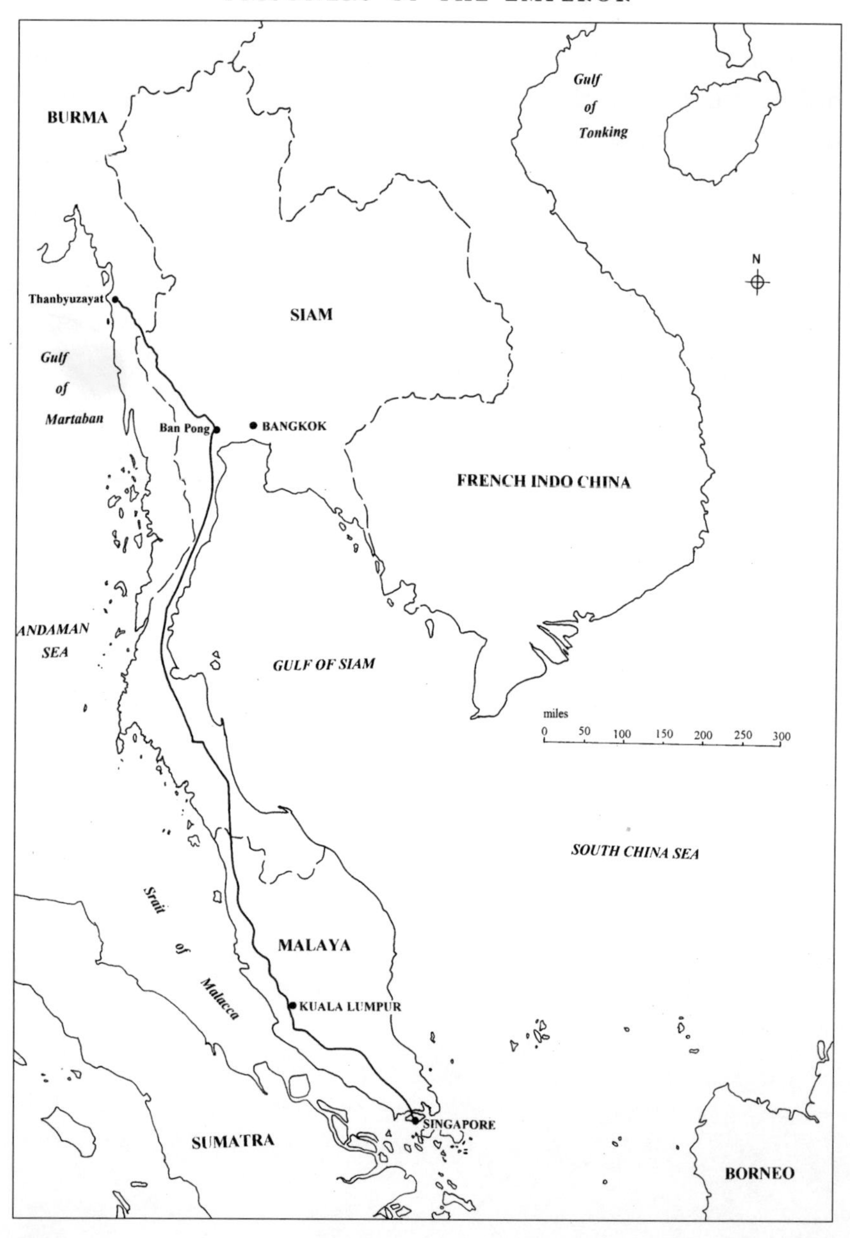

Journey to Thailand

CHAPTER 3

To Thailand, Ban Pong, Wampo

AT THE STATION there was much counting of heads and confusion. Ultimately the men embarked on their journey, thirty to each steel goods wagon, sliding doors open on one side only, and no seats. The wagons were too small to allow all to sit on their kit so about a quarter of the men had to stand on what was to be a four-day journey. They took it in turns to stand. Guards, with a machine-gun, occupied the last wagon.

The sides and roof of the steel wagon, heated by the sun, became hot. Inside, despite being cooled slightly by the breeze resulting from the movement of the train, the men suffered extreme heat. But for the prisoners having managed to persuade their captors to leave open the sliding door on one side of each wagon, they surely would have suffocated. The positions favoured in each wagon were those in the doorway where four men could sit on the floor, with their legs dangling out. Sites near the doorway were the next best thing because the cooling breeze could be felt there also. The worst positions were those where the unfortunate person's bare body was against the wagon wall on the side most exposed to the sun. Requests for change of position were frequent, and sometimes were met very grudgingly.

The train rumbled along at about twenty miles an hour, for hour after hour, then halted. The men poured out, not just to stretch their limbs, but also to answer nature's call. The train had stopped at a small station where lavatory arrangements, for some fifteen hundred men who were in a hurry, were not expected.

And, since the guards would not let them out of their sight they had no alternative but to do their business, whatever it was, on the railway track in view of whomever happened to be present. And since no one had any paper, leaves were used.

The contempt the Japanese had for the POWs enabled them to overlook the need for toilet facilities for their prisoners. Possibly, too, it was another chance for the British to be humiliated in front of the local population. Meanwhile, whilst the wagons were empty, Japanese soldiers had emptied two wooden tubs of boiled rice onto the floor of each wagon for the men to scoop up and eat, because there would not be another stop until six hours later.

After much shouting and counting of heads in each wagon the train was on its way again. By now it was realised that men seated in doorways might fall asleep, and fall-off in a literal sense. Therefore a cord was tied across each doorway, at neck height, so that the man would be awakened if he began to nod off. Those seated there were also more talkative than they had ever been; unusual things are done by men who wish to stay awake to avoid falling off a moving train!

The train stopped every six hours or thereabouts. And the same routine, including defecating on the line and scooping boiled rice off the floor of the wagons, was repeated at every stop. But things were getting progressively worse. Men who could not wait until the next stop had to be held by both arms and both legs with their rear outside the wagon, whilst they did their business. And some now had bowel problems. Despite being very tired, there was no sleep for anyone. They were too uncomfortable and too cramped together, their limbs ached and they were subjected to the continuous jolting of the train and the resultant endless clangs and bangs of the wagons.

Some half-dozen men became too tired to remain alert whilst seated in doorways. They were unable to react quickly enough to withdraw their legs in time to avoid them being smashed against obstructions near the track. Broken legs resulted and the doorways inevitably lost their appeal. After four days of this hell the train pulled to a stop at a small station in Thailand. A barefooted but uniformed man explained in poor English that he was a Thai policeman. He told them that their journey would end at a place called Ban Pong, and from there they would be taken to construct a railway to Burma. He said Ban Pong was not far away.

The prisoners disembarked at the station in Ban Pong, a small provincial town about forty-five miles west of Bangkok. Immediately they were lined up and heads counted. They had become the responsibility of a new set of guards and were subjected to the impatience of frustrated Japanese soldiers who had a communications problem. Then a Japanese officer arrived. He scolded the guards and they became unpleasant and lined up the men again. The officer strode up to the first POW in the line, and made him remove his trilby and hand over the 'V' lodged in the hat band. He stamped the 'V' symbol into the ground. In a matter of moments there was much shouting and face-slapping. POWs were made to remove their 'Vs' and drop them, to be stamped upon. Communication difficulties or not, that Japanese officer knew all about the 'V' symbol!

The POWs were marched away to their transit camp. Dismayed, they saw that the camp site was flooded to a depth of about sixteen inches, the contents of the latrines floating around. The bamboo platforms in the huts, on which the men could rest and sleep, were only four inches or so above water level. The cookhouse was on higher land about three hundred yards away. The area between the camp and the cookhouse was 'no-mans' land, and POWs were required to pass through it quickly. They had to return from the cookhouse to their flooded camp before they could start eating. Conditions in that camp were appalling; the medical officer advised all to leave it at the earliest opportunity. It would be ill-advised of any man to report sick to delay a march if the delay was sought only because of tiredness or being in poor condition. He predicted widespread illness and disease among the men and the longer they stayed the greater the risk.

They were there three days. On the fourth morning, breakfast of the usual poor quality rice, cooked in oil drums into a stodgy mess, was served early. Then, water bottles filled, they began their four-day march towards the distant hills in the jungle. Ian had been issued with a new pair of army boots during the last days at River Valley Road camp. They were a size too large and he had no socks, but then most others did not have socks either. When they left the transit camp in Ban Pong their boots had all been submerged in water, which would not help their feet in the next few hours. The men were weary, not yet recovered from the effects of that rail journey from Singapore, but glad to be out of the filth of their flooded camp in Ban Pong.

The road from Ban Pong, towards those hills, was straight, flat, and flanked by paddy fields. Occasionally there was a roadside tree to break the monotony, but there was no shade for the marchers other than that afforded by their hats. As the sun shone its merciless heat down upon them the marchers were soon strung out over quite a distance; the biggest and the toughest and the fittest strode away from all the others. The guard at the front with them had difficulty in keeping up and, amazingly, there were only six guards escorting the marchers and they minded not that the men were so straggled out. Many stragglers marched in small groups, and the numbers of these groups grew and the distance between groups lengthened progressively. Many men had terrible problems keeping up with their comrades and fell back gradually, eventually to be assimilated into a following group.

Ian was one of those in serious difficulty. The backs of his heels, chafed by the oversized boots, had blistered and the flesh had become so raw that Ian decided he should carry his boots and march with bare feet. His brother Ron had no problems of his own but had slowed and stayed with him, marching at an ever slowing pace. The soles of Ian's naked feet were burned by the road which was heated by the scorching sun; the harsh road surface also tore the soles of his feet, particularly at the crease where the toes joined the soles. A swelling on each side of his groin developed into lumps as large as pigeon eggs. It became impossible for him to stand or walk upright because the tightness caused by the lumps and swelling of his groin caused him nearly to double up to relieve the pressure and the pain there. He tried desperately to continue in that doubled up stance, but could not because he was also quite feverish. Ron encouraged him, but it was hopeless, he could not carry on. He was helped to the shade of a tree near the roadside and lay there; Ron stayed with him. There were already about six others there who had to give up. At the tail end of the march were the Medical Officer and a corporal of the Royal Army Medical Corps and they arrived minutes after Ian had fallen out. Captain Pavillard quickly examined the casualties and reassured them that they would be taken care of; he told the RAMC corporal to remain with them. Then he and Ron were on their way.

By the time a guard arrived some ten minutes later Ian's fever was raging. The guard expressed anger at seeing the men lying down. The medic pointed again and again to the red cross stitched to the sleeve of his shirt, protested bravely and tried to intervene, but the guard would have none of it. He prodded the casualties with his bayonet, put a magazine of rounds in his rifle and screamed at the stricken men. Ian's temperature was raging to the point that he was almost helpless; he was past caring. The medic tried to put himself between the casualties and the guard but was pushed aside. At long last the guard stooped and placed his hand on Ian's forehead and withdrew it quickly. His demeanour changed; he accepted that they were serious casualties who could not march further, and indicated that they could remain under the shade of the tree and that a truck would be along later to pick them up. The medic indicated that he needed to stay with the men, and the guard agreed.

About an hour later the truck arrived. It had already picked up a handful of casualties but none seemed as poorly as this latest group. The medic hitched a lift for a few miles and was subsequently dropped off to join a group of stragglers. Ian propped himself up in the truck, determined to see Ron so that he could wave and show that he was OK. And that he did.

The truck delivered them to a transit camp where they, and the marchers, would spend the night. The camp was tented, and on the edge of a military airfield; other tents in a separate area accommodated a sizeable number of Japanese troops or airmen. Medical officers, and medics from the RAMC, attended the casualties who were advised to lie and rest, because they would be on the march again the next morning. Then the marchers began to arrive and Ian was relieved to see Ron was still in good form.

The usual meal of hopeless rice was eaten, and soon afterwards darkness engulfed the camp. Then a POW who had omitted to acquaint himself with the location of the latrines needed to answer one of nature's major calls. He told his mates what he would do outside a Japanese tent. And he was doing just that when a Japanese emerged from the tent and spotted him. He sought to explain that he had been taken short whilst searching for the latrines. 'I speedo benjo,' he declared helpfully. But the Japanese must have spent some time in America because he shouted in American, 'You . . . Limey bastard. You go and shit on your own doorstep, not on mine. Speedo benjo, my arse,' and then kicked the Brit who was hurriedly pulling up his shorts. It was difficult for the men in his tent to restrain their laughter when the man returned and told the tale. But all knew that he'd been fortunate that the Japanese was civilised enough to kick him in the rear, only in a symbolic fashion.

The Japanese had agreed to an early start for the next day so that the men would be subjected to a little less of the scorching sun. They were up early in the morning, well before full dawn. The damaged areas of Ian's feet had been dressed with lint and sticking plaster but he had no difficulty in putting on his oversized boots. The swelling and lump in his groin had gone but even so he had wisely decided to give his bruises the best possible chance to heal. He planned, therefore, to fall out of the march as soon as he thought it safe to do so, and rely on being picked up by a truck later. He told his brother of his intentions and they agreed that Ron should not hang back with him.

The march set off in the cool of a morning breeze. The hills towards which they marched were shrouded in a mist and seemed as distant as ever. Ian's feet were better than they had been, the cushion of lint and sticking plaster made his boots a better fit, quite apart from the fact that the backs of his heels were protected from much friction. After a mere five miles he rested with a small group of stragglers. Together they decided that at the next roadside tree they would fall out and await events. When the tree was reached Ian removed his boots because his feet hurt, and realised that he'd marched too far. The lint and sticking plaster padding had shifted, the backs of his ankles were raw and his feet swollen. He kept his boots off. Most of the other stragglers in the group had nearly identical problems, but some were also feverish. Untroubled by impatience or apprehension they waited for the truck, but first a guard arrived. He was the same Japanese who, on the previous day, had accepted that they were unable to march further. The previous day's ado was not repeated, he merely indicated that they could rest and a truck would be along later. They completed that day's journey as they had planned, but knew their marching problems were not over.

The transit camp to which the truck took them was again on the edge of an airfield. It was in the town of Kanchanaburi, by the river which was to be popularly renamed the Kwai, near the site where that infamous bridge was to be built. But the men could not know all that.

Medical attention by Captain Pavillard and orderlies was afforded to those who needed it. Many had problems with bruised and blistered feet; Ian's were still a mess, and he had a slight fever, too. At roll-call that evening the men were told that the remainder of the march would be into the jungle, through jungle tracks and pathways. There was no possibility whatever of any casualty being picked up by truck. The Japanese had told the senior British officer that those who fell out would die. The good news was that anyone could stay behind in that camp for three days to recuperate, after which he would have to march. Ian, and many others, knew they had to opt for the three days rest, and then pray that it would be sufficient. He was relieved that Ron said he would stay, too; many others also rested so that they would be there to help their friends in their hour of need. The three days were uneventful.

On the morning of the fourth day the men were prepared for the march, in mind if not in body. Their feet had been doctored as well as possible, they had dried out their boots and liberally saturated them with coconut oil. Ian had drawn a veil over the problems of the first two days of marching and set out with the firm objective of getting to the end of that day's march. All knew that, at least, the jungle offered the blessing of shade from a merciless sun. And it had been raining, so perhaps it would also be cooler.

They set off. Soon they left the metalled road and were on

jungle tracks; they had to march twenty miles into the jungle, and there was no alternative. The monsoons had just about ended, but the jungle paths had not yet dried. In many places, the hundreds who had already trampled that track had made it into a churned sea of mud. Trampling through a jungle, on uneven paths which were obstacled by tree roots and rocks which had broken through the surface of the paths, and the paths themselves sometimes more than ankle deep in churned mud, was a more serious challenge than a march on a flat metalled road, even under a fierce sun.

They trudged on and on, painfully and slowly. In muddy stretches the mud was deeper than the tops of their boots; none had puttees, so the mud seeped into their boots right down to the soles of their feet. And in these stretches it was an effort for them all to lift each submerged foot out of the mud to achieve each single step, such was the effect of the suction upon boots and feet submerged in that morass. Those muddy stretches were frequent and becoming wetter and worse each passing hour, because it was raining. They trudged on, hardly daring to rest because they were making such slow progress. Ian also knew that he should not interrupt his concentration which had fixed his mind on the fact that so long as he kept putting one foot in front of the other he would get there by the end of the day.

The trudge continued painfully, exhaustingly and quietly. The men did not waste their energy, not even on curses or obscenities. Most were disciplined enough to drink sparingly from their bottles, but Ian and some others had finished their water too early, so whenever they passed a pool they scooped water into their tins and drank it. Sometimes the water was green with algae, sometimes tadpoles or mosquito larvae had to be screened out. And the trudge continued even after darkness had enveloped the jungle.

They reached a ravine at the bottom of which a river flowed swiftly. The river had to be crossed by a rope-bridge. The bridge was wide enough for a single file of men, but no one questioned how much weight it could take. Perhaps fortunately, therefore, the men were well separated. Most crawled over on hands and knees in some terror because the flimsy, swaying bridge seemed unsafe to cross in the darkness and rain. And because the swiftly flowing river was some sixty feet below.

Once over the bridge the men had reached their target for the day and were in the transit camp where they would spend the night. It was dark as pitch but they were led by others, with flares, to the cookhouse. They filled up with the expected stodgy rice and then sought shelter in the tented camp, which was in a shallow sea of churned mud. The tents were filled to overflowing; men wishing to squeeze into tents already dense with cramped bodies trying to sleep, were not made welcome. But the latecomers also needed shelter from the heavy and incessant rain, and if at all possible sleep as well because they were spent, and like all there were faced with another killing march the next day. Eventually many had to force themselves into one tent or another, retorting angrily to those already on the inside who were intolerant of their desperate situation.

In every tent the men were in cramped, huddled positions, packed against one another, unable to lie or stretch. And in those conditions they still needed to try to sleep because they knew the next day would be just as awful. But it was worse than that. Throughout the night they were tormented by mosquitoes, at least, in plague proportions, which whined like dive-bombers as they homed in on their luckless prey.

Despite it all Ian must have slept soundly in the end, because all too quickly it was dawn and they had to get up, queue at the cookhouse for rice and then set out on the last lap. All the activity was hurried, almost frenetic, as screaming Japanese impressed upon them the need for urgency; there was no time for medical attention for anyone. Ian had not taken off his boots the previous night, had decided to leave well alone fearing that were he to take them off to attend to his feet he might not be able to get them back on again. At roll-call before marching off, he learned that the camp was called Death Valley, an apt name for a jungle camp dark even in daylight, mosquito ridden and run by frenetic Japanese. The camp was sited on the west bank of the river Kwai Yai, which they had crossed the previous night.

They set off on the last stage of their four day march towards Tarsao, which was on the east bank of the river Kwai Noi, knowing well enough what to expect. They knew they were in a worse physical condition than they had been at the start of the previous day, but they clung to and valued the fact that some time that evening or night, their ordeal would be over. Ian fixed his mind on that, knowing that even if in pain, or near exhaustion, he had to keep on placing one foot in front of the other for the rest of that day.

As expected, the march was similar to that of the previous day, and every bit as terrible, even though they were helped a little because it rained less heavily. It was well after dusk when they arrived at their destination, a place in the jungle called Tarsao. The camp was beside a river. The weary men were greeted with some relief by their comrades who had left them behind at Kanchanaburi four days earlier. The severity of the last two stages of the march had also been a gruelling task for them and they must have worried how their comrades, whom they had left behind, would fare.

The objective having been attained, and the formidable challenge to his morale and to his physical strength met successfully, Ian allowed himself to feel the pain of his swollen and bruised feet and to acknowledge also that he had a slight fever.

The new arrivals ate hungrily and were then shown to their

huts where they were assimilated with their comrades with whom they were reunited. Exhausted and relieved, the men settled down for the night. Probably Ian was not alone in feeling absolute relief that he had reached the end of what was nothing less than a nightmarish four-day march. He was grateful for the help and encouragement given by Ron, but was also acutely aware that had the first two days of the march also been on jungle tracks he could not have survived because there would not have been a truck to rescue him.

They slept well that night; it was the sleep of the exhausted. The next morning Ian was troubled with diarrhoea, but it hardly worried him. At roll-call they were all told they would be taken that day by barge to a place called Wampo which was a few miles downstream of Tarsao, and there they would build a camp for themselves. Then they would start constructing their section of the railway. No time was to be wasted, railway work had to be commenced soon and the men would be allowed only a short time to build their shelters. They were to return to their huts immediately, collect their belongings and then line up again to be taken to the awaiting barges.

Soon the men and their possessions, which had been severely diminished since leaving Ban Pong because much had been discarded during their march, were packed into the barges which chugged downstream. The river flowed quickly between the screens of dense jungle on both sides; the tranquillity of the surroundings was inspiring. It was easy to overlook that behind the screens of trees and the majestic clumps of bamboo reaching fifty feet into the sky and the jungle vines of imposing length, there were jungle tracks carpeted with mud and obstacled with tree roots and rocks, which wended their way through a soggy, mosquito infested territory which was hostile to intruders.

The barge chugged on until they reached their destination,

Wampo; all disembarked into shallow water and waded to a small sandy beach which led to a cleared area behind. This clearing in the jungle, adjacent to the river, was the site for their camp. Some Japanese were already there, with their cookhouse at the water's edge, just downstream of an imposingly built hut on stilts which was also near the river. That was undoubtedly the Japanese Camp Commandant's hut. Not far from it was a much larger hut occupied by guards. Near the water's edge were several stacks of bamboo poles and atap thatching, and these materials were there for the POWs to construct their huts. The site was on high ground and well chosen.

Working parties were organised with some speed and with a great sense of urgency. Some tents were already erected, but clearly these could only accommodate a fraction of the POWs. The Japanese were adept at hut building and quickly instructed the men in these skills. The size, design and position of each hut was specified to the POWs who entered into the spirit of things with alacrity. A party worked energetically on the cookhouse, another dozen men set digging latrines and the hundreds of others worked at constructing POW huts, or were deployed to enlarge the camp site by cutting back the jungle. The men were told they had three days to build their huts, after which all labour would be directed to railway construction.

They worked until dusk, and in some cases continued after dark by the light of fires lit for that purpose. Fortune smiled on the men, and not before time, too. Apart from those who could be comfortably accommodated in the tents, the rest slept in the open under a clear dry sky studded with stars. It was cold during the night, but were it not for the mosquitoes it might have been a very good night for most. But not for all. Ian learned that he was not alone in having diarrhoea; many others were trudging to latrines through the night. None was unduly worried about his discomfort, which in POW language was called 'squitters', a word which had gained usage during the train journey from Singapore. It was an adequate description of diarrhoea, or the dreaded disease, dysentery. It was in its own way a useful word for POWs, because when used by a man with dysentery it helped to trivialise and make that dreaded disease seem less threatening. In time it was used by all, including Medical Officers, who understood the proper usage and usefulness of the word.

Ian was among the fifty or so who had been seen by his MO, Captain Pavillard. Those with seriously sore feet were treated by the medical orderly and the MO prescribed rest to give their feet time to heal. They, therefore, were excused most of the hut construction work. Others told the MO of their squitters, and were given a mixture to settle their stomachs.

Captain Pavillard, who had a Spanish mother and Swiss father, had doctored in Singapore and Malaya before the outbreak of hostilities. He was a brisk and cheerful fellow with a presence which inspired confidence and respect.

On their fourth day at Wampo the POWs' huts were completed, all eleven of them, and they would be home for fifteen hundred men. The huts were of simple design and their assembly and erection presented no problems. The skeleton of each hut was structured from bamboo poles lashed into trusses with thongs of a special stripped bark which had been soaked in water to make them pliable. The trusses were then assembled upright about eight feet apart, each to be joined to the next by horizontal poles. The roof was thatched with atap.

Each hut was about one hundred and fifty feet long and about twenty feet wide; there was a corridor about six feet wide running through the middle from end to end, and the ends of the corridor were open. Additionally there was an opening in the middle of both sides of the hut, so access could be gained from either end, or from the middle. A platform less than seven feet wide, made from split and flattened bamboo poles and raised about twenty inches above the ground, ran the length of both sides of the central corridor, but with gaps for the central exits. The low edges of the pent atap roof reached down to about eighteen inches from the ground, thus eliminating the need for walls along the length of the hut; walls, made with atap, protected the platforms at the ends of the hut, but not the ends of the corridors. The floor was earth.

The space for each man, on which he would keep his possessions and sleep, was less than two feet wide and under seven feet long. The inadequate sleeping space for each man, coupled with the close proximity of the sleeping men to one another, plus the density of the population per hut were, of course, potentially very unhealthy. The huts kept sleeping men dry, but nothing else could be said in their favour.

The hospital hut was about seventy feet long, but of more generous design; the corridor was wider, the roof higher and enabled the sides to be walled, and this provided for adequate height between platform and roof at the outside edge of the platform. The hut, a similar design to that occupied by the Japanese, was bright and airy, which was quite an improvement on the others.

On their fifth day at Wampo the men started work on railway construction, a project to build a railway from Ban Pong in Thailand to Thanbyuzayat in Burma, which was deemed by the Japanese to be a strategic necessity for their forces in Burma. Each morning, immediately after the 7.30 a.m. roll-call, the men were marched in parties led by their guards to the site in the jungle some distance from their camp where they would labour. Initially, an area of jungle would be marked off for clearance each day and the target had to be met before the men could return to camp. The jungle flora comprised a variety of large trees, including fig trees from which hung sturdy vines, and clumps of bamboo reaching forty or more feet high. Each clump had up to about forty canes with diameters of about three inches, and each cane, for its first ten feet or so, was armed with several horizontal spikes about five feet long, and each of the spikes branched in all directions to lock with the spikes of other canes, and the end of each spike, whether the main spike or a branched one, was hard and sharply pointed. Demolishing and removing a clump of bamboo involved considerably more labour and hazards than the destruction and removal of the largest tree, and was made worse if canes were split because their splayed edges had a razor sharpness and emitted a sap which poisoned any cuts inflicted by the bamboo.

In addition to the large trees and bamboo there were smaller bushes and vines, some thorny, some defended by unpleasant substances causing itchiness if touched. Altogether the jungle flora had fierce and formidable defences, and the men had none. Most were clothed only in jap-happies or tattered shorts, many were barefooted, none had gloves or any other protection other than battered hats.

And the trees and the bamboo, when they had been felled, had to be cut into manageable sizes to be dragged away from the designated path of the railway. Teak trees, with their trunks straight and true, were given special treatment; their branches were lopped off and the trunks carried off for bridge construction. Since these trees might be sixty or so feet tall, with trunks having a diameter of two or more feet, their transportation through the jungle was a mighty task. They would be lifted and supported by up to fifty men whilst a rope was wound round the trunk encircling it for its whole length with about thirty loops; then stout poles were slipped through the loops so that about sixty men, in pairs, could carry the trunk with the poles on their shoulders. The weight of the trunk, when it was evenly shared, was not an unreasonable burden. But at no stage during such transportation was the weight ever evenly dispersed between the men; the terrain was uneven, men's heights differed widely and the natural jungle obstacles, mainly trees in the way, had to be negotiated. There was much cursing and yelling by the men crumpling under the disproportionate load they bore, whilst others in a dip in the terrain were unable to take any weight off them until the human centipede progressed further, when tables might be turned. Sometimes, when obstacles were reached, men had to withdraw their poles from the loop, thereby increasing the load borne by their comrades, until their part of the trunk had passed the obstacle. And if the terrain was wet or, worse still, muddy, then the task was all the greater and the hazards to life and limb were considerable.

The tools the men had for their tasks were of the poorest imaginable quality and hopelessly inadequate, so much so that sometimes they wondered how it was that this poverty stricken Japanese army had conquered so much territory. The spades blunted easily, were buckled and bent readily and did not spring back into shape; the POWs seriously thought they had been made from metal cannibalised from oil drums. The axe heads were continually blunted by splitting open at their sharp edge. There were clear indications that their metal was too soft, and they had been fashioned by folding metal over into a wedge shape to provide a hole for the axe handle at the broad edge of the wedge, and the touching edges had been ground down to form a single sharp edge. And that sharp edge splayed open when the axe was used on any hard wood. Axes, if thus seriously blunted, did not simply fail to cut into hardwood, but the swinging axe-man would receive a juddering shock as the axe head bounced off the trunk, and occasionally he would lose his grip of the handle and the bounced axe would become a dangerous missile.

Picks were just as bad. Their heads became blunted or twisted with very little provocation.

The wooden handles of spades, axes and picks gave continuous trouble, wearing away or even breaking where they joined the steel implement. A repair man, sometimes two, was set aside simply to mend or sharpen broken implements, and reunite handles with their metal heads. Inevitably handles became shorter and the already badly balanced implements were more unbalanced and a little more hopeless.

When a sufficient tract of jungle had been cleared some men were assigned to the task of building up an embankment, or cutting away earth to level the track to the height specified by Japanese surveyors, whilst the remainder continued to clear the designated tract of jungle. Moving earth, whether to build an embankment or to cut away to lower the level of the track, was back-breaking work. Pairs of men would dig, throw earth onto bamboo stretchers and then carry the stretcher to throw the earth onto the embankment area, or to discard it. And digging for earth in an area littered with submerged rocks did very little for those picks and spades. Sometimes men digging earth for the embankment would have to dig quite a distance from the embankment, not just because they were not allowed to excavate anywhere near the site of the proposed embankment, but also because the rock strata adjoining the track offered up very little earth to the men, so they had to go further away for it.

Those excavating because the track was too high, also faced formidable obstacles in rocky terrain. Picks, sledgehammers, crowbars and long chisels were overworked. And so, too, the men.

Each morning an increasing number of men attended the sick parade, many with diarrhoea, others with fevers, some with injuries to their limbs. Quite soon many with fevers which had been loosely described as 'jungle fever' were reclassified as suffering from malaria. Some were admitted to the hospital, some were excused work for that day or slightly longer, some were classified as being fit enough for light work, and the rest were given a mixture or some tablets and classified as being fit for duty. The MOs had enormous pressure on them; the Japanese continually demanded that fewer men should be classified as being sick, but there were more and more sick men every day. In effect, the MOs were made to send sick men out to work unless their illness physically incapacitated them. So men who had malaria could be deemed fit for light work as soon as the fever subsided; men with persistent diarrhoea were also deemed fit for light work until they recovered or became too debilitated.

The MOs had other problems too: they had neither the variety nor the quantity of medicines they needed; medical supplies, even simple items like bandages and sticking plaster, were scarce; they did not have the resources to be able to test urine or examine blood or stools; many could not have their ailments diagnosed quickly because of the absence of a microscope. The MOs' use, even of the medicines they had, was constricted because of the need to conserve as much as was possible; so too, the use of sticking plaster and bandages had to be severely constrained.

The first death in Wampo, that of a young soldier in his very early twenties, was caused by dysentery. He was buried in the shadow of the railway track. The entire camp mourned, there was a feeling of much sadness, and an all pervading sense of deep foreboding overtook the camp. There could not be a single POW there who did not realise that many, many more deaths were inevitable because of overwork, malnutrition, disease and the absence of enough medicines. The Japanese provided quinine in adequate quantities, which was a sufficient remedy for most with malaria, but there were those with forms of that fever who needed more than just quinine to cure them, or they were likely to succumb. No other medicines were provided by the Japanese.

But if the men quietly feared the presence of malaria, they felt even more threatened by the prospect of dysentery. Of those with diarrhoea, quite a few had been troubled with it for some time, and its persistence indicated much worse problems than just an 'upset tummy'. Christmas was approaching. They had been in Wampo some six or seven weeks and Ian still had diarrhoea, and had been troubled with it from the day he arrived in Tarsao following that march into the jungle from Ban Pong.

But his stomach problems did not deter him from normal activities, and in true POW fashion he was still an opportunist on the alert for something different to eat.

Late one evening, Ian and Gordon Newman had been required to assist the Japanese cooks to unload some of their supplies from a barge and carry them into the store beside their cookhouse. Included in the supplies were five sacks which the Japanese had allowed to be left just outside the storeroom; they indicated that they would take care of them in the morning. The two men returned to their hut, and there decided that after dark they would raid those sacks.

The two men were not starving, not even hungry, and their planned raid was nothing but an adventure, a kind of dangerous sport. But there was something to be gained from it. They looked forward to the fruits of a sort of lucky dip.

The closest POW hut was some one hundred and fifty yards away from that cookhouse and storeroom, and the track which led to them was anything but secluded. The two men waited until they were confident that the guards had all had their evening meal, then scouted to ensure there was no activity in the cookhouse. Everything was in place, so they set off. Ian's heart was pounding and he wished he had not suggested the raid; and it was sheer stupidity to propose it to Gordon, of all people, who was so adventurous and who never backed out of any challenge. He did not know then that Gordon was having nearly identical thoughts about the escapade in progress.

They belly-crawled all the way from the POW hut nearest to the Japanese cookhouse, commando style perhaps, but without commando skill, speed or confidence. Having started their crawl, and since neither of them had wisdom enough to give way to powerful urges to abandon the exercise, they saw it through to its end. Once there, still on their bellies, they hurriedly untied the top of a sack, snatched some root vegetables, re-tied the sack and belly-crawled all the way back.

They were glad it was all over; neither wanted that kind of adventure again. Their lucky dip had turned out to be some very coarse root vegetables which the Japanese used as pig feed, and which the adventurous duo threw away.

Apart from relishing a challenge, Gordon was also known to be a fitness fanatic extraordinary. His lean, lithe body rippled with muscles of which he was justifiably proud. He had said more than once that the heavy work on the railway was not all bad, because it helped to develop his strength and physique further – but no one believed he meant it. But then, one moonlight night, Gordon was observed doing physical jerks outside the hut, and no one had previously known about his nocturnal exercises. It seemed unbelievable that a man who had spent ten hours each day on heavy physical work should have the need, or the energy, to exercise as well. But it was a bright moonlight night, so his friends dubbed him 'moon man' – but never in front of him, because he was immensely strong.

The man Z, who in River Valley Road had paid others to

smuggle in food for himself and his dog, was in Wampo with his pet.

On the four-day march into the jungle from Ban Pong, he had paid others to carry tins of food he had hoarded and brought to Thailand with him. Men who knew that Z was sharing his tinned food with his dog were hardly pleased by such devotion to his pet. There was considerable resentment that the man's priorities were so inappropriate that he placed the well-being of his dog before that of comrades, many of whom were already feeling the effects of malnutrition. But those who knew the man, knew him to be selfish and concerned only about himself and that which mattered to him. And since he was friendless, only he and his dog mattered to him.

Perhaps inevitably, all his precious acquisitions and the remainder of his tinned food were stolen from him. No one was surprised or even expressed regret. Shortly afterwards his dog disappeared and soon it was disclosed that it had been eaten by those who had stolen it. Z was now entirely on his own, friendless and without any chance of gaining friends because his nature had become well known. No longer with the ability to purchase help, probably also without a single memory of which to be proud, he was in an unenviable situation at a time when every POW knew that in the days ahead there would be a need for help from friends and comrades in order to survive.

At the request of the senior British officer, Colonel Lilly, the camp commandant agreed to grant a holiday on Christmas Day. The Colonel, seemingly an austere and serious minded fellow, was greatly respected and admired by the men; he was a courageous and forthright officer, someone who unfailingly spoke up and got the best possible result for them. He had quickly established a good working relationship with the commandant and each understood the other well. To his men, he was a man of few words who meant what he said and whose overriding concern was their welfare.

The commandant had a surprise up his sleeve. On Christmas morning the IJA declared that, as a gift to the POWs, the river would be dynamited to enable the men to catch the damaged fish. Some six or so sticks of dynamite were exploded in the river and many men then plunged in to retrieve the floating fish. Foolishly, because he was not much of a swimmer at the best of times, Ian was one of those who went in, too. The floating fish were not dead, not even nearly dead; as soon as a swimmer's hand partly closed on a fish it leapt vigorously out of his grasp and shot away several feet, though it remained at the surface all the time. The swimmer, of course, pursued it further into midstream.

Ian had made two grabs at a fish before he realised it was too big for him to grasp successfully; he turned his attention to a smaller one, and then became aware he was further out in midstream than he had bargained for; he also heard Ron and others yelling to him to return immediately. Fortunately for him he heeded their cries and turned for the river bank. He made the bank, but without any strength to spare; for much of the return swim he had struggled against the current, which flowed towards midstream, and knew the situation had become desperate for him. His friends, who waded in to help him with the last few yards, scolded him lest he'd not learned a lesson. He had already realised how near he had been to drowning, had quite a fright, in fact. So a lesson had certainly been learnt: never again would he plunge into the river for a swim if he was seriously weakened by squitters or any other ailment. It seemed a sensible enough lesson because he was more debilitated than he supposed himself to be.

Many had returned with fish. Some had dived in more than once, to catch a second or third or even fourth one, and they were good sized fish too – but they were the more powerful swimmers. Quite a few others had been in a plight similar to Ian's, but had cut their losses and given up rather than be lured into midstream. In total, more than a hundred fish were caught and most men had something fishy to cook on that Christmas Day – either grilled over a small open fire or, if fish heads or tails which had been generously donated, boiled in a tin can.

After his narrow escape from drowning Ian had realised he was weaker than he had supposed himself to be, but he still was unaware just how debilitated he really was. When he had first reported his diarrhoea the MO had prescribed 'medicine and duty', but the mixture had done nothing for his squitters. Later when he reported passing blood and mucus he was given some M&B tablets, but they too, were ineffective; he had then been re-classified as fit for light work only. At this stage the extent of his debility became quite apparent to him, particularly because the Japanese idea of light work was quaint, to put it mildly. The guards persistently demanded of him work which exceeded his physical strength and stamina, but they could not have known he had lost considerable weight quickly.

There was another factor, too. Men with diarrhoea had bad nights every night; their bowels were emptied about every hour; the latrines were about fifty yards from their huts and were a formidable trudge for weakened men. The visits to the latrines were slow in every respect, and painful; the nights were very cold and none felt the cold more than those weakened by illness; sometimes men with diarrhoea did not return to their hut to sleep after their latrine visits, but instead warmed themselves by the camp fire still smouldering near their hut. And their ability to work, or even to remain awake during the day, was sorely tested.

The day arrived when the guard's tolerance of Ian's inadequate efforts at work were tested to the limit. To answer nature's call, he had left the working party and the track, and trudged about fifty yards up a hill. On the way back he sat down intending to have the briefest of rests, but fell asleep, fast asleep. He knew not how long he slept, but was awakened by the guard's shouts. The guard was only a yard away and Ian knew he had to get to his feet quickly because, like all other POWs, he was aware of the instinct of Japanese guards to put the boot in if the POW was on the ground. The guard was much quicker and put in four or five kicks before he allowed him to regain his feet. And then punches, slaps and swings followed. Ian tried to explain that he had to 'speedo benjo', but the guard had caught him asleep and would not believe a word he said. The hitting and slapping speeded Ian down the hill. When they came into view of the working party a sergeant POW interceded and the hitting stopped. The sergeant repeatedly told the guard of his illness, and it seemed as though the message got home because Ian was not harried any more that day. But the guard made a note of his name, which was given as 'Mitchell I.'.

At the sick parade the next morning Captain Pavillard decided Ian should be admitted to the camp hospital.

Ron had had some trouble with another guard some days earlier, and that guard had taken his name too. Ron's name had been given as 'Mitchell R.'.

A few days after Ian's admission to hospital, the brothers' friends reported a hilarious altercation between the two guards whom the brothers had upset. They had been discussing individual POWs, so men nearby listened in as discreetly as they could. The first guard mentioned, among others, that 'Mitchell R.' was 'No bruddy good'. The second guard told him he was mistaken and it was 'Mitchell I.' who was 'No bruddy good'. Each was insistent that the other had got it all wrong and, in turn, Mitchell I. and then Mitchell R. were said to be 'No bruddy good'. The discussion changed into argument, then into angry words, then into a honest to goodness fight in Japanese fashion – they hit one another with bamboo staves. A Japanese NCO stopped them and slapped their faces. The hearing and the telling of that incident was enjoyed by quite a few, and not least by the two young men who had been so maligned; and with every telling the tale was embellished and enjoyed all the more. Ian did not hold a grudge against the guard; he had not been seriously beaten and also thought it likely the guard had not had 'light duties' defined to him, nor could he have known how weakened the POW was. So he enjoyed the tale without feeling sorry for himself. But the brothers were acutely aware the guards might feel they owed them something, so they had to be careful, especially Ron, who would be vulnerable at the track every day.

New Years Day 1943 was marked by the commandant with a gift of fifteen chickens for the camp, and permission for the men to have a concert after the day's work. The chickens were boiled with the usual vegetables, or so it was said, but even those with very sensitive taste buds were not convinced. More than likely all, or nearly all, the chickens were diverted to the hospital; but the fact of any such diversion had to be concealed from the Japanese because they believed in feeding fit workers and had no time for the sick. At Wampo, and in all other camps, the IJA provided half rations for sick men who could not work, and would have been exceedingly cross had they known the POWs shared the rations fairly between all in camp, and if anything special was received it would all go to the hospital.

The concert, lit by camp fires on both sides of the 'stage', was greatly enjoyed. The commandant had agreed that the Union Jack, normally reserved for draping over coffins, could be flown, but stipulated that the Japanese flag had to fly alongside. The commandant was in the audience, at the front beside Colonel Lilly, and all the guards were there too. Somehow, there was a competent band: a bugler of course, someone with a piano accordion, two with trumpets, two with drums, someone with bagpipes. A good vocalist whose speciality was 'Jerusalem', went down very well; so too did the four chorus girls with wigs made from rope and hessian, and busts from heaven knows what; two recited monologues; and all the men sang with gusto during the community singing.

The commandant had ordered that the national anthem must not be sung, so the concert closed with 'Auld Lang Syne'. The men stood and joined in the cross-armed traditional way; the commandant and all his guards rose to their feet quickly and stood with some solemnity, seeming surprised and also pleased. At the end, the POWs and the Japanese learned they had something in common, or very nearly so. The Japanese had risen to their feet as soon as they heard the 'Auld Lang Syne' melody, not because they sought to participate, but because they had mistakenly identified the melody as being that of their national anthem.

The camp commandant was an educated man who had daily conversations with Colonel Lilly and, by all accounts, during those conversations in his hut he was hospitable and sought to portray himself as a cultured person. The Colonel frequently leaked the views expressed by them to one another, and the gist of it all then filtered down to the men. At an early stage in their relationship the commandant told the Colonel that there were a million Japanese soldiers in Burma, most of whom had not yet killed a British soldier and who would dearly like a chance to do so. He said the density of Japanese soldiers in Burma really did make it impossible for any POW to escape and successfully reach the Allied forces; he asked the Colonel to inform his men accordingly as he, the commandant, did not wish POWs for whom he was responsible, to lose their lives.

The conversations were polite and Colonel Lilly was able to

express his views, but on matters relating to the conduct of the war and its outcome, he was careful to avoid introducing the subject; but if the commandant chose to discuss any aspect of the war, or even its likely outcome, then the Colonel said what he thought, and why.

The commandant and the Colonel were able to discuss these fraught matters because the Colonel dealt with the subjects in an academic fashion. Since the commandant was cultured he could accept, or at least pretend to accept, that such gentlemanly discussions were conducted on an academic basis and reflected nothing but the Colonel's judgement. Whenever the Colonel told the commandant of the military and economic reasons why the Allies would inevitably be victorious, the story of what had taken place was eagerly heard by the men in due course. Probably the commandant remained unaware that the Colonel used those conversations to help the men's morale.

The men in Wampo were lucky to have Colonel Lilly who handled the commandant so well. They were also lucky that the commandant was a nicer person than the average Japanese camp commandant. But that did not mean he was reasonable about everything, because he certainly was not. His sector of railway construction was his only priority and he could depend on his soldiers to push hard to achieve the objective without apparent intervention from him. Furthermore, whilst he expressed sorrow about illness and deaths in the camp, he had done nothing about the shortage of medicines, and his concern about the inadequate diet of POWs had merely led to no more than symbolic gifts of a few chickens to be shared between 1500 men. But, at least, he was not an overtly brutal commandant.

One POW, a man who had held a responsible managerial post in Singapore and who had been cheerful, liked and respected in camp, started behaving strangely. He had become very quiet and uncommunicative at first, but now it was worse. The man had developed a compulsion to steal food from the mess tins of others, even whilst they were eating. He would snatch the tin and tip out the rice into his own tin to supplement his own ration. Men learned to guard their food if he was anywhere around – nothing less than a very tight grip of one's tin, whilst also trying to keep it away from him, would do.

He was admitted to the camp hospital where Capt. Pavillard diagnosed vitamin deficiency as being the cause of the problem. The man was then given as much rice as he cared to eat and whatever dietary extras became available. After a few weeks he awoke one morning as his former self. He apologised for his behaviour, said that he had been aware of all his actions but had been quite unable to resist the compulsion. There were smiles of relief all round and all were glad that the man had recovered completely.

Construction of the viaduct at Wampo South had started. A group of men were moved from the main Wampo camp into a small camp on the river-bank opposite to the site of the planned viaduct. The viaduct was to be built to take the railway line round the face of a cliff and above the edge of the river. Each day at the cliff face POWs with long chisels and sledgehammers hammered holes into the hard rock until their guards were content with the depth of the holes. Dynamite was then exploded in the holes to blast away projections and thus to smooth the cliff face against which the viaduct was to be built.

The work was arduous and very dangerous. In the scorching sun, with heat reflected from the whitish rock, temperatures soared, to the point of being nearly unbearable. Men, in teams of three, hammered away incessantly – one holding the long chisel and turning it after each strike so that it was not gripped by the rock, whilst his two comrades swung their sledgehammers alternately –

to drive the chisel into the rock. Guards inserting dynamite into a hole would not permit men working nearby to flee for cover until the fuse was lit and the guards themselves were already in flight. There never was much cover to flee to. Such safety as could be gained could only come by putting distance between themselves and the location of the explosion, and then turning to face that location when the explosion was heard so as to be able to dodge the flying rocks.

Men holding chisels were at considerable risk from the swinging sledgehammers of weary comrades. Accidents were frequent. The tempers of guards were short and high. They were wholly unconcerned about the dangers the men faced – they were enraged when the swinging of sledgehammers slowed in frequency and power because fatigue was overtaking men, and their grip and aim was becoming unreliable. The job was nightmarish and the violence of the guards increased by the day.

On one occasion when the blast hurled a chunk of rock across the river, crashing through the atap roof of a hut in which lay men sick with malaria, the rock crashed into the face of a man, Fitton. His left cheekbone was smashed. A POW was allowed to run along the tract to seek medical help. Capt. Pavillard hurried to the accident and the victim was brought back to the main Wampo camp.

The MO did his best for Fitton, but in those conditions where medical facilities were primitive, the patient finished up with his left eye about half an inch lower than it had been. Capt. Pavillard was confident that Fitton's face could be repaired by surgery after the war. Fitton was a model of courage and optimism and never seemed put out by his misfortune.

A delightful story about an incident in an upriver camp, concerning a raid by some POWs to steal a pig from the Japanese, reached Wampo. In their well thought out operation the men first prepared the setting by telling a story about having seen a tiger one night, its eyes burning, at the very edge of the camp. Everyone believed them, POWs and Japanese alike, so the stage was set for them to acquire a porker. A few evenings later at the camp perimeter, far away from the pigs' enclosure, three of them started a hullabaloo. Their yelling and shouting attracted other POWs, and by the time the Japanese arrived some of the other POWs were convinced that they, too, had seen the tiger. The commandant and all his soldiers were concentrated on that side of the camp, which enabled the others in the plot to seize a pig from the unguarded enclosure which was near the river. After faking damage to the fencing they dragged the pig just a few feet into the jungle, killed it quickly and trailed some blood amongst the trees. The pig was cut up in the dark at the river's edge and the blood flowed away. The rustlers, and many others, enjoyed pork in due course; the truth about the phantom tiger took a few days to spread around the camp.

Coincidentally, just a few days after that tale reached Wampo, the commandant at Wampo organised a tiger shoot. The POWs were arranged into beating parties, forming a semi-circle of men advancing towards the camp from the railway tract; the objective was to drive any tiger, or other game, to the water's edge, where the gallant commandant and his men would be waiting with their guns. The operation was barren. The commandant regretted that nothing was shot, and explained that had the shoot produced any flesh, half would have been destined for the POW cookhouse.

The Malayan currency, earned in Singapore before they were transported to Thailand, had been changed by the camp commandant, who had charged a commission for that service. In Thailand POWs were paid twenty-five Thai cents a day if they worked. At Wampo officers donated a percentage of their pay to the camp hospital.

The string of POW camps for the men building the railway were all located by the river Kwai Noi, which was later to be popularly known as the Kwai. Thai traders in motorised boats brought supplies to the camp, not just rations for the Japanese and POWs, but also other items of food like eggs or peanuts, and tobacco. The amount of foodstuff brought by the traders and sold to the POWs was relatively small, but the supply of tobacco was more than adequate.

Boon Pong was the Thai trader who supplied Wampo and some other camps. The men at Wampo were fortunate to have a POW who spoke Thai. John Pearson, of the SSVF, who had been a businessman in Thailand in pre-war days, made prime contact with Boon Pong. Although Boon Pong could speak good English, negotiations were conducted in Thai so that sensitive inquiries could be made without the knowledge of the IJA. It was safely established that Boon Pong was genuinely friendly towards the POWs. Thus John Pearson was able to pass on to Boon Pong the requirements of Colonel Lilly and the medical officers. Generally the men in the camp did not know how helpful this brave Thai was, nor that he helped to supply money and a small quantity of medicines to the camp. Thailand was a small country, controlled by and at the mercy of the IJA, with inadequate medical resources for its own consumption, so supplies were not easy for him to arrange. John Pearson's involvement, which inevitably placed him in some jeopardy, was not generally known by the POWs.

Since the Japanese permitted only a very few POW personnel to trade with him on behalf of the whole camp, it was easy for the POW administration to retain control of the situation and preserve the required degree of secrecy. But enough was leaked to the men in camp for all to know that Boon Pong was helpful. There was some hope, therefore, that the International Red Cross, which was known to have Swiss representatives in Bangkok, might learn about the catastrophic conditions developing in the railway camps.

Shredded tobacco was sold for about a dollar a hank, which weighed about twelve ounces and roughly resembled a pat of elephant dung, which it was sometimes called; whole leaves were also available. There were also branded Thai cigarettes, the best of which was the 'Red Bull' brand, but they were expensive. Cigarette paper of very poor quality, thick, porous and ungummed, could also be bought; when used, the edge of the paper to be stuck down, if bitten severely and licked heavily, adhered at least temporarily. But it was also necessary to wet the cigarette paper all over, and to do so frequently during the smoke, to counter the porosity of the paper. But for such wetting, which was achieved by licking, air would have been drawn into the cigarette from the length of its outside rather than through its lit end, and the puffing smoker would get nothing for his efforts. And even the licked wet paper was still so porous that the men had to suck each puff with a deep and powerful draw, or else it would all be pointless.

So some men rolled cigars from whole leaves, and this was an adequate solution to the cigarette paper problem, but it was extravagant and inconvenient and did not catch on seriously. Many made pipes from bamboo: for the bowl, a thick piece cut an inch or so above a notch; for the stem, a thinner piece. Such a pipe was possibly better than a cigarette rolled with hopeless paper, and could be made and replaced easily. But bamboo pipes were hot, sometimes they caught fire, and if the stems were not sufficiently long, fire from the bowl was drawn into the mouth; a bamboo pipe lasted for only a few days before its bowl was burned through and its stem was chewed too short. But they could be readily replaced. One or two men carved pipe bowls from hard tree roots and made stems from similar material by burning through with a heated piece of wire, but their patience was hardly justified because the life of those pipes was only slightly longer than that of bamboo ones.

The tobacco was powerful stuff, whether made into a cigarette, smoked in a pipe or rolled into a cigar. The men soaked and rinsed newly purchased tobacco in water to reduce its potency, and that was probably the only 'curing' that tobacco received.

In those circumstances, it should have been surprising that non-smokers took up the habit. But many did, including Ian. And after they became used to that powerful tobacco and could smoke without coughing violently, they were hooked on the stuff and needed it as much as the men who had smoked for some years.

The camp rations, quite apart from being unappetising, even revolting, seriously lacked adequate nutritional value. Rice was the staple food fed to the men morning, noon and night, but it was nothing like the rice which ordinary people eat. Even very poor people in Asia would reject rice of the kind fed to the POWs. The grains were broken, there was more than just a sprinkling of grit present, clearly the rice was the waste swept from the mill floors. It was musty and populated with weevils and maggots, not just a few of them, but so many that every individual serving contained thirty or more of the creatures. The rice was boiled in huge cast iron tubs, without any prior washing and without any effort to reduce wildlife or to filter out the grit. There was neither the manpower nor the facilities in the cookhouse to attend to even such basic necessities. And cooked in huge quantities in those cast iron tubs, stirred almost continually to prevent burning, the inevitable result was a stodgy, gooey mess, a mess with maggots and weevils always in view if one looked at it, and with a musty smell whether one looked or not.

Rice like that, a pint per person, was dolloped into each man's mess tin held in his outstretched hand when he reached the front of the breakfast queue; regularly, there was also a level teaspoonful of sugar served separately so that it was seen by the individual – the sugar was regular, exactly once a week in fact, because the weekly ration of sugar was a level teaspoonful per man per week.

The rice was generally eaten without looking at each spoonful, it was easier that way; but the rice still in the mess tin waiting to be eaten had to be guarded against flies, because bluebottles abounded.

Immediately the breakfast was consumed the men queued again for another dollop in their tin – to take out to the track site for their lunch. By midday, the rice in the mess tins in that tropical heat was partly fermented. Men hoped that fermentation might possibly increase the nutritional value of the rice; perhaps it did, but it was no more appetizing than the breakfast dollop.

The evening meal was a little better, just. In addition to the dollop of rice there was usually a 'stew' poured on top. The stew was boiled vegetables, usually diced pumpkin, or a diced root vegetable of the kind the Japanese fed to their pigs, and sometimes included some strange greens. The total quantity of vegetables was small, perhaps amounting to three or four diced pieces per person, and the watery gravy was only slightly flavoured. There was a shortage of salt, so rice and 'stews' were even more unappetising or revolting than could be imagined.

In Wampo there lived ground lizards which, when they emerged from their small hole in the ground, first poked their heads out and checked that the coast was clear, then scurried at speed to the next hole. And they did this frequently. POWs trapped them to eat by placing a small noose over a hole, and waiting at the end of a string to tug deftly as soon as the unfortunate creature poked out its head. They tasted like chicken, but this delicacy was caught only by sick men who were not at work, and there was some risk to sick men catching lizards if seen by a Japanese. Their logic was uncomplicated: if a man was fit enough to do that, then he was fit enough for work at the track.

The seven with chronic squitters had all become exceedingly thin, so thin that not even the Japanese could doubt they were very ill and too weak to undertake even the lightest of physical work. So Ian felt safe in the afternoons when, with a bent pin on the end of a string, he perched on a log and fished in the river. The bait, a grain of cooked rice, never stayed on the pin long enough for even a nibble. But it was relaxing, he enjoyed doing it and, because he was a supreme optimist, really thought he would make a catch one day.

But it was not to be. A Japanese officer in a passing boat objected. The commandant's attention was drawn to the activity of a man who was unable to work for the Emperor. Inevitably, all sick men were then forbidden to fish. The commandant said it was dishonourable for sick prisoners to have a pleasurable pastime whilst their comrades, and Japanese soldiers, were working hard. He stipulated that sick men should concentrate their efforts on recovery, so that they could return to the service of the Emperor soon.

Since they had already learned so much about the IJA, no POW was even slightly surprised by that Japanese reaction. Those in the IJA, whether officers – presumably with a flawed education which let them believe, among other things, that they were cultured men – or just other ranks whose paramount mistake was to believe all that rot about Bushido and their divine emperor, all had not the slightest idea how petty their minds were.

Camp funds were used for the purchase of a water buffalo for its meat and it was brought to the camp by barge; the animal was old, large and tough. It had to be old because young and fit water buffaloes were valuable to the Thais for work in the fields, and worth more to them for that purpose than was their value if sold for meat.

The Japanese wanted to shoot the animal for the POWs and were to use a former British army rifle, which was heavier and of a much higher calibre than theirs. The buffalo was tied to a tree, its head tight to the tree trunk, and the guard took aim from about ten feet away. Then he lowered his rifle, climbed a nearby tree and aimed the weapon again. But he changed his mind again and passed the rifle to the POW butcher. The man declined to shoot the animal, calculating that its skull might be too thick to be penetrated with one shot. He slew the animal with an axe, and the guard climbed down from his tree when it was all over. The camp enjoyed a meat broth the next evening.

A serious sanitation problem developed and grew progressively with each passing day at Wampo. The latrines, which were open trenches about eighteen feet long, five feet wide and ten feet deep, were a breeding ground for bluebottles and other flies. Within a few weeks after the latrines came into use there was a carpet of maggots covering the bottoms of the trenches; these maggots, larvae of bluebottles, soon covered the walls of the trenches and subsequently carpeted the area of ground for some six feet or so surrounding the latrines. It was, of course, unpleasant to have to walk through those maggots. And all, excepting those trodden by the men, grew into bluebottles and seriously threatened the health of the camp.

The camp sanitation party consisted of about four men whose daily task was to dig latrines, or fill them in, or dig drains around the huts to channel rainwater away, or to tackle any similar problem. A junior lieutenant, a man called Bushell, stepped forward to lead the sanitation party in the battle to eliminate bluebottles, or at least to end their free breeding.

Lt. Bushell was a professional soldier who had risen from the ranks; almost daily he visited the hospital and spoke to each patient, cheerily and optimistically he sought to tell them to cheer up. He did his best, but was well out of his depth and had not realised that most sick men understood their perilous situation, were keenly aware of the importance of maintaining their personal morale and were already quietly engaged in their own private battles. They tolerated the young officer, believing him to be a man who was proud of having been commissioned and who sought to behave as a leader of men should. But his reward for all his efforts was to be nicknamed 'Bullshit' Bushell, and the nickname was bestowed upon him by his former regimental mates whom he had left behind when he was commissioned. Nobody disliked him, it was evident to all and sundry that he meant well even if his efforts were not appreciated, but the nickname implied some ridicule, and seemed appropriate at the time.

But 'Bullshit' proved himself to be a better man, and a better leader of men, than most. The commandant had decreed that every POW in camp not engaged on railway construction had to kill one hundred flies daily, and the flies had to be counted and surrendered to prove that the target was achieved by all of them. That meant that the cooks, the sanitation party, the sick and the officers, a total of about eighty men had to kill and hand over eight thousand flies daily. But flies being short-lived, their numbers might not be reduced much, if at all, if killed perhaps only hours or a day before their natural life span expired. It was also probable that eight thousand was only a fraction of the number of maggots which developed into flies each day. The only real solution was to end the conditions which permitted them to breed so freely. And 'Bullshit' Bushell planned to do just that.

He took charge of the sanitation party, did as much of the manual work as any other man there, and won their respect and admiration. He planned the replacement of existing latrines with fly proof ones; he designed bamboo covers for trenches, commodes with lids, all made from bamboo and which would fit over openings in the trench covers. He rightly believed that flies would not enter a darkened latrine trench. Colonel Lilly was impressed; he persuaded the commandant to increase the number of men authorised for maintenance of sanitation and to allow Lt. Bushell a free hand on the project he had planned.

The sanitation squad, with 'Bullshit' leading it by example and with genuinely exuberant enthusiasm, dug the new trenches and made the new latrines more quickly than seemed possible. Because of the brief life span of flies it was only a few days after the last of the old latrines was filled in that the bluebottle problem was virtually over. Other camps, of course, had the same sanitation problem. 'Bullshit's' remedy was passed on to them, and in camps where the commandants agreed to increase the number of sanitation workers the problem was overcome. Regrettably, not all commandants were reasonable or responsible people, so there were camps which remained fly infested for as long as they were occupied.

As for 'Bullshit' Bushell, in time all who came across him spoke highly of the man who had risen from the ranks, was selfless and courageous in his concern and defence of the men during the blackest days of railway construction, and who cheerfully knuckled down to give practical help whenever he could. The nickname 'Bullshit' Bushell, sometimes shortened to 'Bullshit', was avoided in his presence though it continued to be used, but as a term of endearment rather than one of ridicule.

The fly problem was resolved, but in addition to the swarms of mosquitoes which descended upon the hapless men each night, two other infestations developed which could not be satisfactorily countered, and which plagued all POWs in Thailand for the rest of their captivity.

The first of these to appear were bugs, which lived and multiplied in the splayed bamboo platforms on which the men slept. It was impossible to eradicate them; the cracks and crevices of bamboo and atap were a perfect habitat, and the men sleeping only inches from their lair, a convenient larder. Whenever possible the men removed the splayed bamboo slats and exposed their undersides to the sun which destroyed many bugs. But most survived because of the crevices and cracks in which they could shield themselves from the sun, and those housed in the atap roofs could not be got at in any way; and they bred and multiplied rapidly. From dusk to dawn bugs emerged to feed on the sleeping or lying men; and they, restless in their uncomfortable sleep, tossed, turned and slapped themselves wherever they felt a bite, whether from mosquito or bug. And when a bug was squashed the reward for the man and his neighbours was a sickly smell which faded only slowly; inevitably, the smell of squashed bugs pervaded the huts throughout every night.

And through the nights, in addition to slapping sounds and the whines of attacking mosquitoes, men uttered groans, pleas, curses and expletives, not just at the mosquitoes and bugs, but also in demands to their neighbours to keep still, or to straighten up, or to shut up. Men, worn and tired by long hours of heavy work, or sick with fever or dysentery, deserved and needed more rest and more sleep than these conditions could ever permit.

The other infestation to plague the men in those camps was lice. They lived and multiplied in the seams or rough edges of clothing, even in jap-happies, and in the jute rice sacks which all used as blankets. Blankets of any kind could be seen to be heaving with lice if left out in the sun, but the lice were not killed, they simply moved into shaded areas of the material. Lice fed on their victims in daylight as well as at night, leaving the garment to crawl onto the victim and then bite. They had tough skins, and a man feeling a bite would pluck the louse off him and squash it between the backs of his thumbnails until it burst.

The jute sacks and the seams in men's garments concealed hundreds of lice eggs which adhered fiercely to the material, and it was hardly feasible to physically destroy them. Drowning the lice was tried; men submerged their sacks or garments in the river for half an hour or longer, but afterwards, within a few minutes of exposure to air, the lice revived. As with mosquitoes and bugs, lice remained with them throughout the rest of their captivity.

During the concerted attempts to drown the lice, men kept their jap-happies on for prolonged spells in the river so that fish could also pluck off the lice, but fish weren't interested in lice and instead nibbled at the cuts and sores on bodies and limbs, particularly sores with pus or rot of some kind. One naked man, in the water up to his chest, held out his jap-happie below the water to drown the lice, or for fish to eat the lice, or failing that for the current to wash out the lice – 'a sort of treble chance', he had said . He had the misfortune to have his penis severely bitten by a fish, which was a chance he had not considered. His greater misfortune was that when he went to the medical orderly for treatment it was decided that all in camp should be warned to protect themselves against such attacks, and the episode and the man were subsequently the subject of much mirth.

The Japanese had soap and ample bathing opportunities; they had daily opportunities for their clothing to be washed and for their bedding to be aired in the sun; they had clothes to change into whilst their washing dried in the sun; they had plenty of space in their hut and did not have to sleep cheek by jowl as did their captives in their densely packed huts. Therefore it was rather stupid for one of them to remark to a group of POWs, 'English soldier dirty,' when he saw a man pluck a louse off his stomach. The remark was reason enough for the POWs to see to it that the Japanese were also subjected to infestations. Live bugs were transported to the Japanese huts whenever possible and many a POW retained lice plucked off his body to flick onto Japanese whenever opportunity arose. And thus was born the idea of doing unto the Japanese all that was possible, which led to the sparing of the lives of centipedes, scorpions and a whole host of other unpleasant creatures which abounded in the jungle, so that those creatures could enjoy some of the space in the Japanese huts. The scorpions were large black ones whose sting could be lethal – it was not simply that the men were vindictive, they also enjoyed the total challenge of capturing, containing and concealing the venomous creatures until they could be released in the precincts of the Japanese hut.

The first anniversary of their capture, 15 February 1943, arrived – it seemed much more than just twelve months since the surrender, it seemed a very long time indeed. The men were mostly in thoughtful mood, not despondent, but there was a deep sense of foreboding throughout the camp. How would it all come to end? Would the war end suddenly and in a way that would enable them to be spared from massacre? Would it even end in time to save them from the ultimate consequence of malnutrition and disease, because those were pressing threats? No one doubted that the Japanese would get their comeuppance in due course and some of the men would have done a deal with the Devil just to stay alive long enough to see that day. And Ian sometimes thought that way, too.

Captain Pavillard's hospital had some thirty or more patients. Seven with chronic squitters, another few with beri-beri, most with malaria, some dying of cerebral malaria, some with fevers, some with ulcerated sores, one out of his mind because of vitamin deficiency and one or two with civilised complaints like appendicitis or stomach ulcers. A handful had already died and were buried in a patch – in the vicinity of the railway tract – which had become a cemetery with crude wooden crosses. Among those who had already died was a sergeant major, a big and friendly fellow and a thoroughly nice man who had been kind to all he met. The MO had known he was dying, but the other patients had been surprised by his death and were shocked and greatly saddened. In the hospital, death was not usually private: the discomfort and ugliness of death, its sounds and even death's smell were there for the patients to see and know as it was happening. There were no screens, nowhere to move men to so that they could die privately with some dignity, no chaplain to comfort and reassure the dying. As a general rule men died slowly over a period of hours, but even though amid their comrades and without seclusion, they generally died alone, uncomforted, because all in the hospital were chronically sick men who knew of their serious peril and found it difficult to cope with death in their midst. They could cope only by gazing away from dying men because the need for the preservation of their personal morale seemed to demand of them that they be remote from death in all its ugliness.

After his daily round of patients, one morning Captain Pavillard called on the seven men suffering from chronic squitters. Outside the hut he addressed them in serious tones. He told them they had not responded to treatment of bacillary dysentery, and since they all had chronic stomach pains and diarrhoea and continued to pass blood and mucus, it was his view that they had amoebic dysentery. He told them the drug to treat that disease, emetine, was not available in any POW camp in Thailand – he had caused enquiries to be made and the response was universal. In other camps, too, men had amoebic dysentery. The Japanese had been pressured to supply the drug and had refused. They had also refused to approach the Red Cross in Bangkok.

He said it was up to each of them to endeavour to slow down the ravages of the disease as much as was possible, and to hope circumstances would change so that the drug would become available for them. He advised the avoidance of abrasive foods, of fibre, of anything which contained solids. He said rice was OK in that context and as much of it as possible should be eaten. Fluids from boiled vegetables or from meat or fish were OK, but generally the substance should be avoided. There were exceptions: for example, pumpkin-like vegetables when boiled to a pulp could be eaten, but the skin had to be avoided. He told them he considered that, with great care about their diet, they could hang on for some time. He wished them all good luck and told them to hope and pray.

Ian and his six comrades had already concluded that they had dysentery and had wondered why they had not responded to the M&B tablets which had cured some people of their dysentery. They had been unaware that there was more than one type of dysentery bug, but now they knew the true score. In silence they returned to the hospital hut and did not discuss the matter among themselves. Ian did not want to take part in any possible discussion because he did not wish to hear any pessimistic view. And probably the other six felt that way too. But he, and probably all of the other six, was instantly aware that whilst the MO's recommended dietary restrictions might slow down the ravages of the disease and reduce the stomach pains, it would aggravate the malnutrition problems every POW faced. That the MO had said nothing about that, and had not indicated whether they might hang on for days, or weeks, or months, must also have sunk in.

Among the seven were two rugger players whose prowess on the field, when they had represented Singapore against Service teams before the Japanese war started, had been much admired. Douglas Seward, the lanky winger with long and powerful strides, was now a stooping man whose ribs could be counted from a distance; Joe Potter, the squat and sturdy scrum half whose seemingly bandy legs had not hindered him in his terrier-like game, had become a thin, small, stooping figure, his slightly bowed legs seeming devoid of flesh. Ian could only shake his head and know not what to think. But it did occur to him that the absence of mirrors in the camp, except for tiny ones, was no bad thing. Then he dismissed such thoughts from his mind.

That night when Ron visited, Ian told him what Captain Pavillard had said. Ron remained silent; they both realised the full implications of the prognosis, and each knew the other would not welcome any concealment or optimistic pretence. Ian kept to himself his resolve, already made, to do all he could to hang on; he told himself he might not have to outlast the hostilities, there must be some chance that at any time, when least expected perhaps, the Red Cross might be allowed to bring medicines to the POWs. He knew he had to remain optimistic and hopeful, it was his only chance.

Ron continued to visit the hospital most nights, but there were times when he could not make it because the workday had lengthened. The daily quota of work on the rail track had increased progressively; the task set for building the rail embankment, or cutting away to level the track, had been redefined and increased to one cubic metre of earth, or rock, moved per man day. Given the inadequate and poor quality tools the men had, and the rocky terrain, the task they faced had become physically demanding to the point that it was unrealistic. Those building the viaduct round the face of a cliff edging the bend of the river at Wampo South, faced monumental demands on their strength and stamina. They did not have a measurable quota to meet, they were simply driven by shouting, screaming, violent guards.

The Japanese had realised railway construction had fallen behind the schedule demanded by the military requirements of their forces in Burma. Their need to catch up and then maintain the rate of progress set by their strategists boded ill for all POWs in those camps. 'Speedo', the word shouted by guards to hurry up men working, had been used more and more insistently, more demandingly, and was being enforced by violence. The horrendous period of railway construction, which all called the 'Speedo', had started. The Japanese decreed that chronically sick men, unfit for work, were to be moved down river to a camp called Chungkai.

They said it was a hospital camp. Since the Japanese intolerance of sick POWs who could not work, exemplified by halving their rations, was a fact which none could overlook, their cynical use of the word 'hospital' cut no ice. The news of this decree was broken by Captain Pavillard to the seven men with amoebic dysentery. He said they would be moved downstream by boat the next morning and assured them there were British medical officers in Chungkai camp. He added that the Japanese had promised good medical attention, including medicines, but advised the seven he knew that their promise of medicines for them in Chungkai was a lie.

The seven, all members of the Straits Settlements Volunteer Force, were visited individually that afternoon by a Captain in the SSVF. He was serious and grave, there were no trivialities and no attempt to suggest the men might be better off downstream in a non-working camp; the seven appreciated the honesty of both him and Captain Pavillard. He told Ian that Colonel Lilly had sought to persuade the commandant to allow his brother to be moved to Chungkai as well, but the request had been turned down.

That night Ian wondered if the commandant, and his cronies in the other camps, had learned of the nature of amoebic dysentery through Captain Pavillard's request for the drug emetine and, having been told that the sick men would not recover and be available for work until they received the appropriate course of injections, had decided it was time to get them out of the way.

Early the next morning, almost before the full brightness of dawn, Ron called to wish his brother good luck. As he watched Ron leave to join the breakfast queue, Ian wondered if they would ever meet again. Probably Ron had similar thoughts. After breakfast the seven, accompanied by Captain Pavillard, made their way to the small pier. Colonel Lilly and the SSVF captain were there to see them off; the seven boarded the Thai motorised boat, accompanied by a harsh and unpleasant Japanese guard who was over eager to get going. The boat chugged off and within a minute they were out of sight of their former camp. The seven were the first group of seriously sick men whom the commandant at Wampo got rid of because they were spent and useless to him. They were: Douglas Seward, Joe Potter, Donald Hare, Bill Dobbs, Johnnie Keay, Grahame Gardiner and Ian.

Just half a mile or so downstream they passed the viaduct being erected against the face of the cliff which was at the river's edge. Seen from the river, it was an amazing scene: three hundred or more men toiling at constructing a stilted railway viaduct, with teak tree trunks hoisted upright, their feet embedded into the rocky terrain at the foot of the cliff, to form the stilts upon which the upper structure of the bridge was being built. Stability was achieved by leaning the construction into the face of the cliff. This major undertaking was being achieved by men with ropes and pulleys, hammers and chisels, axes and saws, picks and shovels and dynamite. There was not a crane in sight, nor any other mechanised equipment. The job was already more than half done and the completed viaduct could easily be pictured in the mind. It was unlikely that any in the boat would choose to be on a train chugging across that unsafe contraption when it was completed.

The boat entered the bend of the river downstream of the South Wampo viaduct, ending their last view of Wampo and the POWs slaving there. They had but just started their journey to Chungkai.

CHAPTER 4

Chungkai

SEVERAL MILES AFTER LEAVING WAMPO SOUTH the boat stopped at Wanian POW camp, which was thought by men in upstream camps to be called 'One Lung'. The guard hurried them out of the boat; it was a severe climb up the steep and slippery bank, but he was intolerant of the men's problems and voiced his impatient anger at their slowness. They were able to speak to one resident POW and he had time enough only to tell them the name of the camp. The guard walked them through the camp and onto a path which took them to the railway line, about four hundred yards away from the edge of the camp. They could see that the railway had been completed up to a little beyond that point because materials like sleepers and railway lines had been brought there by rail; bogeys were loaded with some of the materials for movement further up the line.

The men boarded a diesel engine lorry which was fitted with rail wheels and were escorted by the same miserable guard, who might well have been unhappy because of his proximity to very sick men, the nature of whose illness he did not know.

Several miles on the journey neared its end when the truck passed through a cutting and stopped at a simple wooden platform. The men left the truck and were walked to Chungkai POW camp. The camp had been a railway construction camp but, when the line had been completed well past Chungkai, most of the men had been sent to other camps up the line to work. Some were left behind for maintenance work on the railway, and for loading rail trucks with materials to be sent to Wanian and beyond, as the line progressed.

The new arrivals were met by a medical orderly who took them to the place in a hut which had been assigned to them. He told them they would all be seen by the MO that evening, or the next morning; they were told where to queue for their food, and the location of the latrines. He pointed out the direction of the river where the men could bathe and wash their garments. He explained they were not in a hospital; the MO would not normally visit men in these huts, they could attend sick parade, which was held each morning, if they needed to see him.

They soon learned of the sorry state of Chungkai camp. The fit workers were in the huts nearer the river. Most of the other huts, which comprised the greater part of the camp, were dilapidated and leaky; the latrine trenches were open and dirty, in some cases the walls were crumbling, in all of them maggots abounded, they were up the trench walls and also on the surrounding ground. If ever a place needed a man of 'Bullshit' Bushell's calibre, then surely that place was Chungkai in early 1943 – particularly the dreadful part of the camp occupied by the sick. The overriding problem was that the Japanese would not provide enough fit men to maintain adequately the entire camp. Insufficient fit men were made available to cook, look after sanitation, maintain the huts, tend the very ill and dig graves; they could only do their best. But the outcome had to be that conditions would deteriorate further. It was difficult to avoid the conclusion that, worse than being merely unconcerned about the welfare of the chronically sick POWs, the Japanese welcomed their worsening living conditions because it would hasten the deaths of men who were now useless to them.

The men learned they were among the first of the chronically sick to be sent to Chungkai. The hut they were in was empty

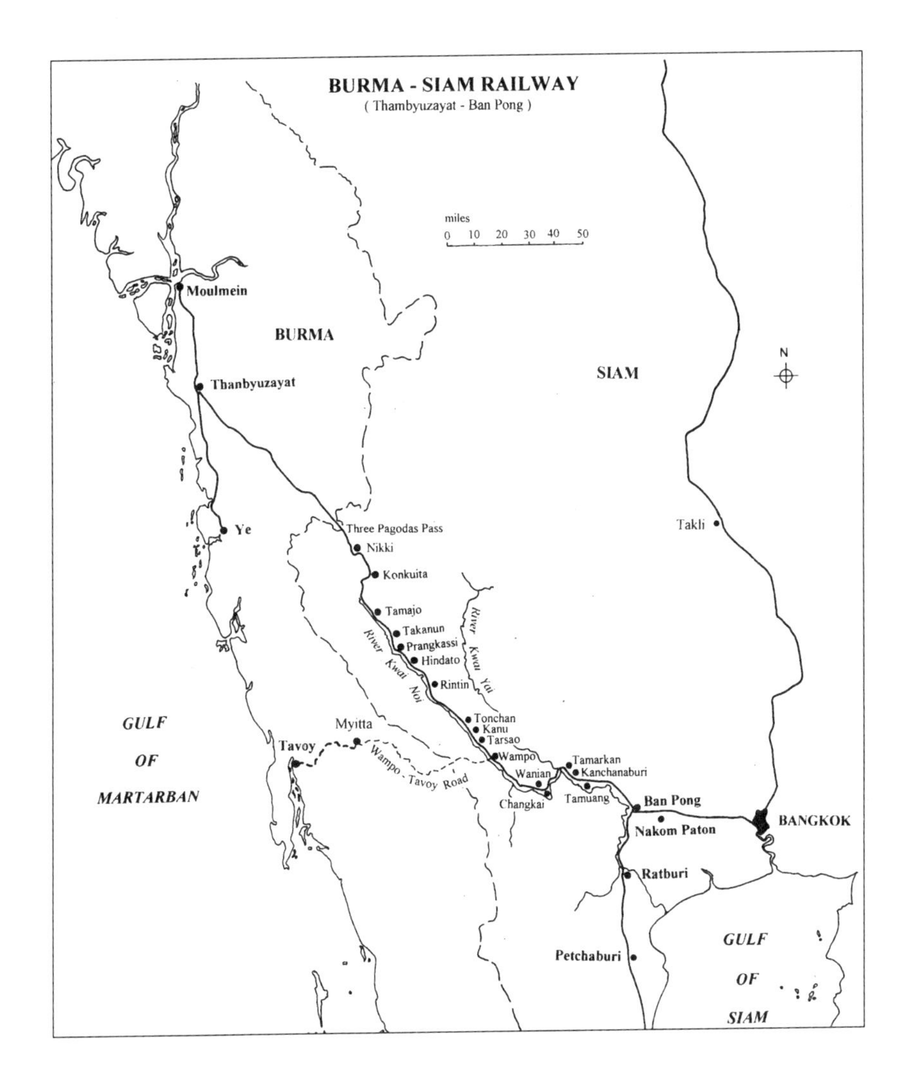
BURMA - SIAM RAILWAY
(Thambyuzayat - Ban Pong)
miles
0 10 20 30 40 50
N
Moulmein
BURMA
Thanbyuzayat
SIAM
Ye
Three Pagodas Pass
Takli
Nikki
Konkuita
Tamajo
Takanun
Prangkassi
Hindato
Rintin
River Kwai Noi
River Kwai Yai
Tonchan
Kanu
Tarsao
Wampo
Wanian
Tamarkan
Kanchanaburi
Changkai
Tamuang
Ban Pong
Nakom Paton
BANGKOK
Ratburi
Petchaburi
GULF OF MARTARBAN
GULF OF SIAM
Myitta
Tavoy
Wampo - Tavoy Road

but for them, so they were able to spread out a little to avoid the spots where rain dripped from the leaky roof. The next morning they attended the sick parade which was held immediately outside the hut. The MO explained that Captain Pavillard had diagnosed amoebic dysentery and, from their symptoms, he had no reason to disagree with the diagnosis; he said that there were no microscopes in Chungkai but efforts were being made to get one. He said he would walk through their hut each morning and would gladly see anyone who needed him; they need not attend the sick parade to be seen by him.

The MO had successfully reassured the men. But there was a substantial difference between the conditions in Wampo and those at Chungkai. In Wampo, latrine hygiene was good; the river, where walking patients could wash, was just a few yards from the hospital hut; Captain Pavillard knew each of his patients; the hospital hut was airy, new and did not leak; the sick in Wampo were in the same camp as their regimental comrades, among whom they had personal friends who could be relied upon for such help as was possible. Chungkai had none of those advantages, and the food – which was half rations – was inevitably far more inadequate and of worse quality than previously known. Chungkai had one more telling disadvantage: chronically sick men were present in Chungkai in greater numbers, and in greater proportions, than in Wampo. There were considerable cumulative disadvantages in having an inadequate ratio between fit men and the seriously ill, and this was particularly so in the conditions which existed in those camps.

After only a few days in Chungkai it seemed that most of the seven from Wampo had lost ground more rapidly than previously. Probably they all noticed it. Ian knew his own spirits had declined, and scolded himself; he realised that the stress, including the physical strain their bodies had been subjected to during their move to Chungkai, had contributed to the worsening of their squitters and their tiredness. He rationalised that he would regain the lost ground and that he had thoughtlessly allowed himself to worry unnecessarily. That little, and seemingly insignificant, episode typified his personal and perpetual struggle to preserve his spirits; whenever they fell a little he knew he had to regain them, and usually did do by rationalising events.

Daily, more sick men were brought to Chungkai, some by boat and rail, some all the way by boat. Mostly they were men with amoebic dysentery; or with huge ulcers on their limbs; or with serious nutrition deficiency illnesses like beri-beri or pellagra; or cerebral malaria. With very rare exceptions, every POW in all the camps regularly had malaria, and that disease therefore was additional to other illnesses which the men had.

The men who arrived daily included Australian and Dutch POWs. Most POWs on the railway construction were British, but there were sizeable Australian and Dutch contingents also. To a great extent the men sent to railway construction camps were initially sent there within units, thus at Wampo there had been a sizeable number from the SSVF and other British units, and none from Australian or Dutch units. But Chungkai had become a melting pot for all. The Dutch had been captured in Java; the Australians were from units captured in both Singapore and Java.

Mick Coombes, a twenty-two-year-old Tasmanian who had been captured in Java, was a new arrival in Chungkai, and became one of Ian's friends. His space in the hut was beside Ian. On the other side of Mick was another Australian, Mike, who had been a tin mining engineer in Malaya, and had been conscripted into the SSVF. Both of them also had amoebic dysentery and it seemed that there was little, or no, difference in the medical condition of the three. Soon the three were buddies.

Mick was a particularly nice person, pleasant, considerate and with a naturally friendly disposition. He had been a tailor before joining the Australian army, was uncomplicated and unassuming. Mike was older and more serious than the other two, but they got on well.

Ian had acquired, by stealing it, part of the inner flap of a Japanese tent and had planned to make himself another jap-happy. Mick suggested that he should make a pair of shorts instead. Not just shorts with a drawstring waist, but a tailored pair with fly buttons and all. They unpicked part of a kit bag to obtain 'thread' and Mick provided a needle which he had fashioned from a key type tin opener from an old sardine tin. Mick explained the shapes required, showed how they should be measured and provided a battered pair of scissors. He kept a watching brief on progress as Ian measured, drew, cut, assembled, tacked and stitched. Mick had the required degree of patience to instruct without taking over the work which engrossed his young friend; he never expressed impatience. It took about a week to produce the finished article, but time had been unimportant. What was important was that neither of them, even briefly, wondered if their patience and dedication were justified.

The shorts were a success. They were loose, because they were planned on the basis that the shorts should still fit Ian even after he gained weight in the weeks which lay ahead. And in planning the loose shorts, there never was any thought other than that; there was no question of pretended optimism, it had simply been a matter of elementary common sense. Ian was proud of his effort and, given any encouragement, would have paraded down the hut gangway to show them off!

Almost daily, sick men from upriver railway construction camps continued to arrive in Chungkai. The somewhat dilapidated and leaky huts in the hospital area of the camp filled up rapidly, and soon the sleeping space per man was barely two feet wide. Bugs, lice and mosquitoes abounded. The state of the latrines and their precincts deteriorated progressively with the increased usage, particularly because so many of the users were dysenteric. A man with dysentery could be expected to visit the latrine between twenty and forty times a day, and sometimes visits were left until too late, particularly during the night. The paths from the huts to the latrines were continually soiled by sick men who badly needed a bed-pan service, but Chungkai then had very few medical orderlies and the Japanese would not waste their fit POWs on such unproductive work. No arrangements existed even to cover the accidental messes with earth – so overworked were the few orderlies that even such imperatives had to go by default.

The carpet of maggots surrounding each open latrine trench grew ever wider. Sanitation and hygiene were an almost insurmountable difficulty because, in the absence of toilet paper, or any paper at all, leaves were used. The river was about four hundred yards away and therefore out of reach of these sick and weakened men; they did not have buckets or cans to catch and hold rainwater, so their hands remained unwashed until it chanced to rain. When it rained the men washed their garments and themselves, but generally without soap.

A medical orderly, who had escorted a barge load of sick to the camp, offered to carry messages back with him to upcountry camps. Mick gave Ian part of a Thai cigarette packet so that he could scribble a note to his brother. The intention was only to let Ron know that he was alive and kicking, but the message he wrote advised Ron to stay away from Chungkai if at all possible because of the filthy conditions.

The sick men seldom, if ever, saw a Japanese. The IJA stayed well away from the sick and from their part of the camp, with all its disease, filth and squalor.

The men with amoebic dysentery whom Ian knew seemed to

be losing ground at a rate which should have worried them all. Ian was certainly concerned about being so much weaker and thinner and about the increasing frequency of his visits to the latrine. Then one morning when he awoke he was unable to stand upright; his visit to the latrine was made on all fours. Quite apart from wondering what had happened to him, the journey was unpleasant because of the filthy path and the need to pick his way through. Before returning to the hut he rested away from the path and decided that he should stay there for a few hours, at least, to reduce the number of long crawls to and from the latrine, which would have been required of him about every hour. Then he sensed that that would be the first step down the slippery slope which would lead him to giving up completely. He knew he must put up with this latest difficulty and see it out. The alternative was to give up, and he had set his mind against that weeks earlier.

His return to the hut was greeted with questions from his friends. They had seen him crawl out and had wondered what it was all about; they had not expected him to crawl all the way there and back. They reassured him that probably he had got his back into a poor posture during the night and strained a muscle, or trapped a nerve. Whatever it was, they convinced him it would be very temporary. They were right, because only that day and the next were non-walking days for Ian, as on the third day he awoke to find the problem gone. But those crawls to the latrine and back were later to cause him nightmares.

Additional MOs had been sent to the camp, enabling each of them to look after fewer patients. Consequently, the MO in charge of the dysentery hut was able to devote more time to each of them. Some days after Ian's trouble with his back, the MO, on his morning round, stopped by him and without much ado decided that he should be hospitalised. The hospital ward was a better place to be in than the dysentery hut: each man had about twice as much space for sleeping; the queue for food – for those who could walk – was shorter; the latrines were closer and their precincts were kept clean; an orderly was available if needed; the MO saw each man every morning; water was available for washing hands; there was order rather than disorder in the hospital ward and the roof did not leak. During his stay there, Mick and Mike were also moved in, so the three were together again.

After some three weeks Ian was returned to the dysentery hut. Whilst in the hospital ward he had not received any medicines, but his stay had helped him and he seemed stronger, though still very, very thin. Mick and Mike remained in hospital and Ian visited them often.

Several men had been discharged with Ian. The reason for the clear out may have been because of a surge of sick POWs who had arrived by barge. Many had dysentery, many had deep ulcers on their limbs, all were in a dreadful state because they had been crammed into the barges; some had died on the journey.

The new arrivals had terrible tales to relate. They told of how the 'Speedo' had so intensified that men had to slave for sixteen hours of each and every day, working at night by the light of fires; of being awakened each day well before dawn, of eating their breakfast and being marched out to work still before dawn, of not having seen their camp in daylight for several weeks; of how cholera was present in every upriver camp, of the agony and death of scores of its victims; of sick men being forced out of the camp hospitals by bamboo wielding guards for work on the track, some having to be carried there because they could not walk; of the daily task for building the embankment being raised to a metre and a half per man day; of manic Japanese; of beatings and killings of those who failed to do enough; of the Kanu Kid, the Black Prince, the Silver Bullet, the Mad Mongrel, the Works Master, the Tiger and of a whole host of other brutal, murderous guards.

Men who had been sent downstream to Chungkai during the early days of the 'Speedo', and who thought they already knew all about Japanese brutality, listened in shocked silence at the horrendous litany of inhuman treatment meted to their comrades upstream. They all had friends, even brothers, in those upstream camps, and were instantly aware that those horrors were still going on in all of those camps, even at that moment. They were told that many hundreds of men had already died.

Those who listened to the newcomers were themselves desperately sick and debilitated men – all of them only a little more than skin and bones – who had already been in Chungkai for some weeks, and who had previously cursed their luck for having landed in that hell hole. They sensed that their misfortune had saved them from much worse hells. Ian, dazed and not knowing what he hoped to find, toured the hospital huts to see if Ron, or any one else he knew, had arrived.

One of the new arrivals in the dysentery hut was another member of the SSVF, a man nicknamed 'Mexican Mitch'. He, too, had been in Wampo. It was there that he had been given that name – because his surname was Mitchell and he had made a Mexican looking hat from a straw rice sack, and also to readily differentiate him from the Mitchell brothers. His appearance, small and with a dark beard, was a bit Mexican, but he never enjoyed the nickname; still less did he like being dubbed 'Mex', which abbreviation was often used. Ian also had a dark beard but was lucky enough not to have a Mexican looking hat!

Cholera struck in Chungkai soon after appearing in the upstream camps. The swollen river had carried the disease to all the camps it serviced, and it had become suicidal to bathe in its waters. All water had to be boiled before it was safe to drink, even rainwater. Men bathing in the monsoon rains were advised to keep their mouths tightly shut to ensure that not even a drop filtered into their mouths because of the possibility that the falling rain itself might be contaminated as it dripped through trees or off the roof of huts.

Men struck down by the disease were stretchered to a tented area outside the camp boundary. There they were laid under mosquito nets so that flies could not get to them to pick up and carry the germs back to camp. Brave medical orderlies tended them in their tortured suffering as they dehydrated quickly with diarrhoea and continuous vomiting. Their bodies contorted with cramp, they screamed and groaned in agony. The first indication of cholera was vomiting, and within just a few hours of those first symptoms the victims usually died of dehydration and exhaustion – the cholera bacteria were normally expelled from the body by the diarrhoea and vomiting.

After the initial outbreak the MOs organised the preparation of sterile water collected from contraptions set up to make and collect sterile steam. The sterile water, dripped into the victim's body, alleviated the extent of dehydration, and about half the victims then survived the disease itself. But the survivors had been so weakened that many subsequently died from any illness which might afflict them, and since almost everybody had regular bouts of malaria they remained vulnerable for some time afterwards. The cholera season was at its height during the monsoon rains when floods washed filth into the swollen river, and the bacteria then threatened all whom the river serviced. Then the flies which were always around picked up the bacteria from filth to intensify the spread of the disease.

Because of the exceptionally high death rate claimed by cholera, and of the agonies suffered by its victims, it struck real terror in the hearts of POWs in railway camps. Despite a man's hunger he would unhesitatingly throw away the remainder of his rice if a fly settled on it, or even buzzed his mess tin. Certainly the disease caused more intensified pain and was more devastating to its victims than any of the other diseases which plagued so many.

There were others, too, who suffered great pain. Men with tropical ulcers, which grew wide and deep in the limbs of about two hundred in Chungkai, were tormented with pain and tested severely over a period of weeks. These men, mostly with leg ulcers, occupied a hospital hut adjacent to the dysentery hut. The ulcers had developed from scratches, cuts and wounds from accidents, or from beatings with splayed bamboo, which was poisonous. The cuts and wounds could not be treated or cleaned, or protected with bandages or plaster, because there were none of those basic supplies available, and because the unfortunate men still had to work long hours in the jungle. The nutrition deficient diet had run down the ability of men's bodies to fight infection or naturally to heal their wounds.

The men in that ward were in severe pain with very little, if any, medicine to treat them. There were not even bandages to protect the rotting flesh from flies; banana tree leaves were used for that purpose. Medical orderlies tended them as best they could and scraped away at the rotting flesh and maggots with spoons whilst others comforted and restrained the patient during the painful daily ordeal. The men with ulcers were run down and debilitated; the ulcers contributed to their weakness not just because they sapped strength, but also because the men with such ulcers were in considerable pain all the time. The pain, when coupled with the stench of rotting flesh which pervaded that hospital ward and the surrounding area, made hopeless rice even more than normally unappetising. And when gangrene eventually set in, the limbs were amputated. There were instances where men pleaded for amputations before that stage, to end their torment.

Captain Markowitz, a Canadian, saved many lives by successful amputations in seemingly impossible conditions. Using the crudest of tools, with limited anaesthetic and medicines, surrounded by orderlies with fly swats, he amputated away. Some men died because they had become too weakened to stand the rigours of the operation. The surgeon decided that amputations had to be carried out at an earlier stage – that it was too often fatal to delay amputating until it was certain, by normal standards, that the limb could not be saved.

Amputations were a daily event and in the course of a few weeks afterwards, active and very cheerful men swung themselves around camp on bamboo crutches. And, of course, their numbers grew with each passing day. The surgeon was renowned and respected in Chungkai and all admired his wisdom and courage in going for early amputations; they had absolute confidence in him. Therefore those who prefixed his name with the term 'Saw-Happy' did so in jest.

Something was happening to Ian's body – or mind – he knew not what to think. His appetite for food had gone almost completely and it had become necessary for him to force himself to eat, so repulsed by the food had he become. He was greatly troubled because he knew the consequences if sick men, already only a little more than skin and bone, ceased eating even if only for a few days. He had watched men die when they had given up and stopped eating because they had lost the will to live, or so he had thought. It was with the greatest of difficulty and only after stoic determination that he was able to put into his mouth, then swallow and keep down, just one or two half spoons of rice at each meal. He could not chew the food – it repulsed him too much – he had to swallow it quickly. And it became worse on the fourth day when he was not just repulsed by the sight of rice, but also by the sight of men eating it. At breakfast time he could not bring himself even to get his rice and force down a spoonful; he just lay on his bed with eyes shut so that he could not see others eating. His friends realised he had stopped eating and was troubled, but were helpless.

During the morning he built up a resolve to queue for the mid-day rice and to eat two spoonfuls, to compensate for his failure to eat any that morning – because he had earlier made a bargain with himself to eat at least one spoonful per meal. When the mid-day rice queue formed he delayed joining it until near the end when the queue had shortened considerably, because he knew he was too weak to stand for long. The mid-day sun was hot and there were about ten in front of him in the queue, on open ground just a few yards from the huts; he repeatedly felt on the verge of fainting through weakness, and squatted to minimise the fall if he blacked out. The man behind him, not realising what it was all about, scolded him, so he stood and moved forward a pace or two to close the gap in the queue before squatting again; this was repeated three or four times before he reached the men doling out the rice. Then he rose again with mess tin in outstretched hand. The server noticed something wrong, and asked, 'Are you all right, mate?' The effort had been too much for Ian and he blacked out. His light frame fell to the ground before he could be supported. They carried him to the nearest hut, the dysentery hut for officers, and he came to as they laid him down on an officer's bed. He was ashamed because he was instantly aware that his jap-happy was soiled during his blackout, and there was now a mess on the bed. He apologised, but the officer was kind and was anxious about the well-being of the young man, above anything else. He escorted Ian to his hut and told his friends what had happened. Ian did not eat anything that mealtime either, but it had been a valiant try, even if a total failure, and he did not reproach himself. He did down a spoonful in the evening.

Ian's friends, particularly Grahame Gardiner and Bill Dobbs who were two of the seven who had come to Chungkai from Wampo with him, had given much encouragement in the preceding days when they first realised that something was wrong. They had also urged him to attend sick parade, believing that the MO might be able to help. But Ian had steadfastly refused, without explaining the reason for his refusal, which was that he could not see how the MO could possibly help since he thought his revulsion for food was a psychological matter rather than a medical one. That evening Bill Dobbs told him he would attend the sick parade the next morning, even if it was necessary to drag him there. Since there was nothing to lose, and he also knew now that he could not fight his losing battle on his own any longer and needed help desperately and urgently, he said he would attend. In any event he knew Bill to be a fiercely determined man who spoke his mind forcefully when occasion warranted, and his words could wound; but much more than that, he was a man Ian had grown to look up to as a worthwhile role model. Ian was glad to have the concern of those two men.

Bill escorted him to the sick parade and told the MO all he knew; Ian was not trusted to say a word, in case he did not tell the whole story. The MO knew immediately what was wrong, but pulled down Ian's lower eyelid to confirm his diagnosis – he had jaundice. The MO told them both that he would continue to be repulsed by food, excepting very sweet foods like jam or syrup, until the jaundice receded on its own. Unless he could get sweet foods, there was no realistic chance that he could down rice on its own. He asked Bill if he, or any other friends, could get hold of some jam or golden syrup. Bill shook his head.

Ian and Bill were greatly relieved as they heard the MO's prognosis: Ian, because he now knew the cause of his inability to eat and that it had nothing to do with his mind; Bill, for much the same reason. They returned to their place in the dysentery hut, and there were smiles all round. But Ian knew that if he was unable to start eating soon he would lose ground so fast that survival would be unlikely. He could not avoid reflecting on the number of occasions when he had unjustly assumed that many he had watched die slowly, had died simply because they had stopped eating from choice.

Just before the mid-day meal Bill returned after a brief absence from the hut. He gave Ian a tin of strawberry jam with strict instructions to eat every bit of the jam himself, saying that none of it should be shared. He refused to say where it came from, saying he could not do so; and he never did disclose who made the gift. A spoonful of jam with rice at each meal enabled him to eat almost all his ration of rice for the next three days; then the jaundice faded as rapidly as it had arrived, and Ian was bright and cheerful again. But he was thinner, much thinner than before the jaundice episode began, and had much ground to recover.

At the time Ian believed the gift of strawberry jam almost certainly saved his life; he never had cause to alter that opinion and remained grateful to the generous donor whose sacrifice, in the conditions existing at Chungkai at the time, was indeed a generous one.

Names of men who had died in the upcountry camps arrived in Chungkai and it had been decided that the list be read out to the men in all huts. It was the middle of a dismal and rainy monsoon day when the list was read out by an officer to the men in the dysentery hut. Each name read was followed by the man's rank and regiment, and he read slowly and distinctly to minimise the risk of confusion and mis-identification by any listener. It was indeed a sombre gathering; every man in the hut collected together around the officer, listening silently and shocked. None was surprised by the length of the list, having been warned in advance by the officer, and in any case, the recent sick arrivals in the camp had already told them that hundreds had died. Ian listened intently and anxiously, hoping his brother was not on the list, and was relieved when the officer reached the end. He knew some of the men named, including Charles Peel from his platoon, the factories inspector who had been with him in the River Valley Road camp in Singapore, and Captain Parr, the chaplain, who had been the vice-principal of St Andrew's School, Singapore.

He was saddened by the news. He had watched men die, in Wampo first, and then in Chungkai, and death had become a daily occurrence in Chungkai. He, and probably almost everybody else, had become at least partly inured to the deaths of their comrades, excepting the deaths of particular friends. That did not mean they did not care much if those who died were not their particular friends – they cared deeply, as was evidenced when the first deaths occurred at Wampo. But their senses had since been numbed by the scale of it all. It seemed to Ian that a defence mechanism clouded their minds to obscure the dreadful facts, but did so less efficiently when the victims were close friends. He told himself that probably everyone felt as he did, and that he was as sensitive as any to the horrendous events taking place; that whilst the list was being read, others were almost certainly also concentrating their attention on hopes that particular friends were still alive.

Some days had passed since Ian's jaundice had cleared and yet he had regained nothing of the weight he had lost. It had not occurred to him that men with chronic dysentery should not expect to regain any lost weight until the dysentery was cured and the wasting away was ended – and this was particularly so because their diet was so inadequate. He was admitted to the hospital ward again, which surprised him because he had not attended a sick parade for quite a few days. He wondered if a friend had anything to do with it, but was glad enough to go in. A microscope had been obtained by the hospital and within a day or so it was confirmed that he did indeed have amoebic dysentery.

He was located in the same ward as his two Australian friends, Mick and Mike, who were just across the gangway almost opposite him. He had not seen them for two or three weeks and had to conceal his dismay that they were much weaker than he had expected them to be. Their voices had also weakened considerably.

Ian had been to the river for a wash and he thought the exercise might also be good for him. The river was about four hundred yards from the hospital hut, but he had walked slowly and rested frequently. At the river, he had stayed by the water's edge because in his weak state he knew he would be at risk were he really to venture in. A man had realised that he felt insecure and stayed with him until he left to return to the hospital ward.

When he neared the hospital, the path passed another which led to the mortuary where a sergeant major was about to lead off a funeral party, consisting of himself and four bearers. Ian saw the group, but did not take in what was happening because his mind and efforts were concentrated on walking back to the hospital. The sergeant major shouted, demanding that the disrespectful soldier show some decency to the dead. He added that it looked like it might soon be his turn to be buried, and he would not like it if he was then shown disrespect. Ian was taken aback at first, but regained his senses quickly enough to realise that he should ignore the further shouts of the lout, disregard the unpleasant fellow completely and continue his return to the safety of the hospital. He also made a mental note that if such men were deemed good enough to become warrant officers in the Regular Army, then he would never seek a career in the army.

A few days later the hospital ward, which was in a low lying area of the camp, was flooded. The patients were moved into tents hastily erected on higher ground. Ian and his two Aussie friends were together in the same tent, with about ten others. The MO, Major Black, did his round of the tents each morning, but his visits seemed to be largely routine because he was severely constrained by the shortage of medicines. On about the fourth morning in the tent, when the MO reached Ian, the accompanying orderly said, 'This is Private Mitchell, Sir.' Major Black asked the usual routine questions about the frequency of his visits to the latrines, then carefully told him that the orderly would give him an emetine injection later that morning, and another one the next day. He said the orderly would break open the phial containing the emetine in his presence immediately before the injections, and that the MO would ask Ian about the injections on the morning after he received each of them.

When the Major left the tent Ian was confused by a mixture of strong emotions. Of course he was overjoyed about the prospect of being cured of the debilitating disease which had been with him for about twelve months. He knew perfectly well that without the emetine he would die, probably within weeks. But all in the tent had amoebic dysentery, including Mick and Mike whose conditions were worse than his, and there was no emetine for them. His predominant feeling was that he was overjoyed by his good fortune, but his joy was more than just slightly tarnished by the knowledge that he alone, in that tent, had been favoured by good fortune. He knew he had to subdue the extent of his relief in the presence of the others in the tent, but he was inexperienced in the art of tact and subtlety and knew not what to say. He could not hide a guilty feeling about trying to conceal his great joy, even though that joy was genuinely qualified.

He need not have worried so much on his own. Mick quickly sensed his difficulties and came to the rescue, and Mike helped, too. 'That's wonderful news, Ian. I'm glad for you,' he said, and Mike agreed. Then others murmured assent. But Ian still felt he had to suppress his joy which, to him, now seemed indecent, even obscene. He could not seek refuge outside the tent because it was raining; he had to remain and face the difficult human experience which he was ill equipped to cope with. Mick again came to his rescue. It seemed he knew the emotions and difficulties his young friend was experiencing. He told him it was a good day for him and he should enjoy the news; they did, so why not he? Ian mistakenly felt it necessary to explain he was sorry all the others were not also getting the medicine, and that spoiled things for him. Mick said there was always a tomorrow, and then things cheered up.

The orderly arrived and gave Ian his injection. The tent returned to normality, excepting that Ian, though immensely relieved and with a sense of great, though qualified, joy, still felt that in common decency he had to conceal his happiness. And the only way he could do that was to keep his mouth shut as much as possible.

The next day during his morning round, Major Black asked if the injection had been given in the way specified. Ian confirmed that it had. The MO reminded him that another injection would be given him that morning, following the same procedure. And so it was, about an hour later.

On the following morning the MO again sought confirmation that the injection had been given as he had specified. He also asked if the emetine had started to work. Ian had longed for that question. 'I think I'm a little constipated,' he said, with a happy grin. The MO was pleased but advised him he had been given about half the recognised dosage only, that was the most anyone at Chungkai would ever get, but it should make the disease dormant. A full course of injections, to effect a final cure, could await the end of the war.

Ian knew he would remember for ever the events of the last few weeks, and in particular the last few days. Obviously he would remember because the emetine was a life saver for him. But he also could not forget that his two Australian friends, whose illness was more advanced than his, would instantly realise their chances of recovery had been written off by the MO, since they had needed the emetine more urgently than he did, and yet had been passed over. That had been the overriding reason why he had felt so badly about being joyful when he had been singled out to receive the injections.

He later learned that medicines were being smuggled into camp, but emetine was difficult to get in Thailand. A decision was therefore taken by the senior MOs that emetine, when available, should be given only to men with an urgent need for it, and then only to those for whom it seemed certain that the recipient's life would be saved by half the recognised dosage. The need to maximise the benefit of drugs, particularly emetine, placed an onerous burden on the MOs. Therefore in the immediate aftermath of receiving emetine, those fortunate to be exactly sufficiently ill when it was available, probably felt a responsibility to take greater care to ensure their subsequent survival.

Generally it was supposed that someone was venturing out of camp after dark to bring medicines in, though the man's identity was not known to ordinary POWs. Those fortunate enough to receive life-saving medicines which had been smuggled in could never forget their debt and, in the meantime, could only pray that the brave person would not be caught. But Ian, in common with almost everyone else, was unaware that in Chungkai more than one brave person risked his life in the clandestine operations to bring medicines and money into the camp. One of them, Corporal R.C.H. 'Johnnie' Johnson of the SSVF, a former British businessman in Thailand, spoke Thai. From within the camp precincts, he arranged for money and medicines to be concealed within the sacks of rice and vegetables being legitimately brought in. Two other men in the SSVF, whilst out legitimately on rations detail, arranged for money and medicines to be concealed within the sacks of incoming supplies. A medical officer in the Federated Malay States Volunteer Force, who was allowed out to make legitimate purchases, also played a part. But all this was a well guarded secret.

A week after his second emetine injection Ian was discharged from the hospital ward and returned to the dysentery hut. All in the hut had been required to supply specimens for microscopic examination and those who were shown not to have amoebic dysentery were expelled and sent to a workers' hut. There were more than a score of such men who had sheltered in the dysentery hut by deception. Some others remained, having been furnished with specimens by their dysenteric friends, or having bought such a specimen. Those with the bug, including men like Ian whose dysentery had become dormant, were kept in the hut and became designated as members of the Amoebic Battalion. As carriers of the disease, it was decreed that they should remain separated from the rest of the camp; in particular, the Japanese kept well away from that hut and its precincts. The members of the Amoebic Battalion now had the privilege of being in a kind of sanctuary; their good fortune was envied by others who naturally enough sought admission to that battalion. It became necessary to warn the battalion that any person caught supplying a specimen for another man to submit for examination would be expelled and sent upriver at the first opportunity. And so the trade in specimen stools was stopped at a very early stage.

On a visit to his two Aussie friends, whose deterioration had continued slowly, Ian was told by a smiling and happy Mick, 'You're going to be all right; I can see flesh on your shoulders; you're going to make it. Good on you.' Mike also smiled and nodded. It was clear that his two Aussie friends knew their days were numbered, that there was no chance whatever they could live much longer. Ian knew their pleasure at seeing his physical improvement was spontaneous and genuine, that all three were aware he was OK now, and that all three were equally aware Mick and Mike would die. There was no need for him to feel badly about the situation – he had two remarkable friends who wished him well, and whose friendship he valued and would never forget. Some days later Mick and Mike died, within the same hour. Ian's sadness was relieved by knowing that their sufferings in pain and squalor were ended and they had died in peace with themselves. But more than for any other previous deaths he had known, he felt theirs to be a great waste. Subsequently he often wondered if either of them would have survived had the emetine been given to one of them instead.

At this time some thirty or so men were dying each day; the causes were mostly amoebic dysentery, cerebral malaria or malnutrition. Small and forlorn funeral processions were led from the mortuary, through the camp, to the cemetery on the other side of the camp site; the processions could be seen from the hut occupied by the Amoebic Battalion and the subsequent bugle sound of the Last Post was listened to in the hut in a still silence, and what went on in the men's minds was always unsaid.

A captain in the officer's hut gave Ian a small job so he could have some money to spend. All that was required of him was to carry a four gallon can of water from the river to the officer's hut, once a day, for the officer to wash in. Ian knew that he had been given the job to help him because a canteen, run by Thais, had been started up in camp and items of food could be purchased if one had money. But the effort to carry the water some three or four hundred yards was too much for him. It was only with the greatest of efforts that he could carry the can for about ten yards before it began to slip out of his fingers; so he stopped and rested frequently. And it was not just that he had insufficient strength in his fingers, hands and arms, but the strain on his stomach muscles worried him considerably. After three days he thanked the officer and explained that he was not up to it; the captain was sorry and said he had given him the job believing that it would help him.

Ian subsequently spent many idle moments wondering if it really was right for officers to employ batmen in those POW camps. Was it not enough that they were paid more than a dollar a day whilst men earned just twenty-five cents a day only if they were fit and worked; why did many behave as though their duty was discharged by donating one tenth of their income to the camp hospital, and that any subsequent monetary help given by them had to be worked for? Did they not appreciate that they were also better off than the men because they had more generous living accommodation, shorter queues and, quite importantly, their clothes and boots lasted longer because they were not subjected to the full rigours of work? Ian had little doubt that he was unsuited for any military career; his view was that leaders of men should instinctively be fair to the men they led. He thought that in POW camps there was a shortage of evidence of that important quality.

Conditions in camp had improved considerably since the early days when Chungkai had become a dump into which the Japanese had cast chronically sick men from upriver camps. More fit men were now in the camp, sanitation was much improved and the Thai-run canteen was in heavy demand by those who had money. There was even a well run barber shop where men had their hair cut and beards trimmed by POWs for a small fee. Things looked even brighter when, for the first time since their capture twenty months earlier, Allied reconnaissance aircraft began to appear in the distant skies. This, the first indication the men had of Allied war efforts, suggested that the tide was being turned and the enemy halted. An optimistic request to the Japanese that a red cross or some other sign be displayed for aircraft to see, was turned down. But the men were unconcerned, having confidence that their presence in Thailand to build a railway would already be known to the Allied forces, and the camps near the railway could easily be identified from the air. In that assumption the men were entirely correct and those camps were never directly targeted.

Officers and men from the Amoebic Battalion were generally prohibited from the precincts of the cookhouse and canteen, but arrangements existed for a handful of them to collect buckets of food from the cookhouse to take to the dysentery hut to be doled out. And two men were authorised to enter the other ranks part of the canteen to make purchases on behalf of the others in the battalion. One man, Ian, was authorised to make purchases from the officers' part of the canteen on behalf of the officers in the battalion; the queue in the officers' sector was always shorter than that in the other ranks sector. Captain Riley, a twenty-two-year-old former public schoolboy, for whom Ian had much respect and liking, collected the individual orders from his fellow officers to pass on to Ian each day, and subsequently received the purchases to distribute. Ian was happy to have this duty; it was lighter and less unpleasant than some other chores which the men in the hut were sometimes assigned.

The arrangements worked well for some weeks. But one day a sergeant major, the one who had shouted abuse when Ian had failed to salute a nearby funeral procession, noticed him in the queue in the officers' canteen and challenged his right to be there. Ian sought to explain, but was shouted down by the uncouth fellow. The sergeant major raved, demanded that the soldier should stand to attention and call him 'sir'; asserted that he had no right to be there on two counts: he was not an officer and men from the Amoebic Battalion were forbidden to use the canteen. Ian refused to be humiliated, stood his ground, explained and then angrily told the sergeant major he was mistaken, adding that he intended to remain and be served because he was acting under the orders of Captain Riley whose orders took precedence. The sergeant major, looking as though he would burst, said the soldier was under arrest and in serious trouble. An officer intervened, telling the sergeant major that the correct thing to do was to ask the soldier to report immediately to his Captain Riley, for him to deal with the difficulty. He instructed Ian, kindly and firmly, to return immediately to the amoebic huts and inform Captain Riley of what had happened.

Captain Riley was angered when Ian told him of the treatment meted to him by the sergeant major. The Captain strode to the canteen, taking the young soldier with him to identify the sergeant major, but suggested that it would be wise for him to remain just outside the door, where he would be able to watch the proceedings. The Captain at first spoke quietly as he explained the approved arrangements for the purchasing of orders for officers in the Amoebic Battalion. The sergeant major mistook that civility for weakness and challenged the Captain's statement. He used bluster, too, saying that the officer was mistaken and everyone in the Army knew that other ranks were prohibited from officers' messes excepting to serve or scrub the floors. In the presence of the thirty or so officers there, and in the full view and hearing of about sixty men in the other ranks sector, the now fiery Captain dressed down the sergeant major. And the happiest observer of all was the young soldier standing in the doorway.

Subsequently the arrangements were reviewed. Ian was then required to queue in the men's sector of the canteen to satisfy protocol, it was said. Others thought the sergeant major probably had the ear of the senior officer in camp who had been persuaded that, in the long term interest of discipline, the sergeant major's authority had to be reinstated after his public dressing down by Captain Riley. Ian knew that it would be very much in his interests to avoid confrontation with that sergeant major in future. He fervently hoped for the man's continued good health so that he would never join the Amoebic Battalion.

Oliver Hartley, a former plantation manager in Malaya, was a newcomer to Chungkai who quickly realised the advantages of being in the Amoebic Battalion – and promptly joined it. His younger brother, Dickie, had been a member of Ian's platoon but was missing in action two days before the surrender. Oliver told Ian that news had since been received that Dickie, a dispatch rider, had strayed behind enemy lines and been captured and executed.

Oliver – who had another brother, Melville, a corporal in Ian's platoon – knew Ian well, and both were glad to have one another as friends when they discovered each other in the Amoebic Battalion. Oliver was very fit, shrewd and streetwise, and therefore a useful buddy to have. Within just a few days of his arrival in Chungkai he had learned his way about and made the occasional after dark excursion to the nearby Thai village to bring in food and drink, but mostly drink called 'firewater' because of its potency. It was said that firewater contained some wood alcohol, but that meant nothing to Ian since he had never had the chance to learn about alcohol because of a strict upbringing.

He had regained much of his lost weight and had decided to get rid of his beard and look more presentable. Oliver knew where a stainless steel table knife, with a blade cut to half its original length and sharpened to a razor edge, together with a sharpening stone, could be purchased for a modest sum. So Ian bought them and became clean shaven. Each shave, which was of course soapless, had to be interrupted four or five times to renew the edge on the blade, but they could afford the time. Ian preferred to shave his friends rather than risk allowing them to harm the blade by careless re-sharpening.

Christmas 1943 was just a few days away and Oliver mentioned his plan to bring in some firewater. He joked at Ian's expense, remarking that he had never been drunk, never had a girl friend, never smoked a decent cigarette and, like everyone else there, would probably be dead before the war ended. Foolishly Ian walked right into the trap and agreed he would drink firewater on Christmas Day if Oliver could give him enough to make him drunk, and in return he would give Oliver a Christmas shave. Their friends in adjacent bed spaces, particularly Grahame Gardiner, looked forward to the event with much merriment.

At about ten o'clock on Christmas morning Oliver produced a half bottle of firewater and poured some for Ian, who asked if it was enough to make him drunk. Oliver said, 'Yes, providing you drink it quickly,' and there was much laughter. So Ian, who had never refused a challenge in his life, never welshed on a bet and never been drunk, now never gave himself a chance to think this was a good time to concede discretion was more sensible than stupid valour. He drank the stuff in three or four gulps; it burnt its way down his throat, and he thought, 'I know why they call it firewater.' A crowd looked on in amusement.

Immediately the liquor was downed he remembered his obligation to shave Oliver for Christmas, and picked up the sharpened knife. Oliver fled. He tried to reason with those who urged him to put down the knife, even offering to shave them for Christmas, but whomever he offered to shave simply fled. He tried to chase one or two, so that he could discharge his part of the bet, but they must have been fitter than he was, because they ran more quickly than he could. Then he collapsed with a spinning head.

His relieved friends carried him back to his bed space, and there he moaned, groaned and regretted he'd been so foolish. He vomited and vomited and vomited for a seemingly endless day. He was aware of the concern that his loud vomiting might be heard by any passing guard, with consequences which might be serious. He was aware that Sergeant Major Cobb, who was in charge of the hut, was urging his friends to stifle the vomiting noises by submerging his head under hessian rice sacking. Time went by and he continued to vomit and moan and groan until late in the evening and well into darkness. He was aware his friends were concerned that, if discovered by a guard, cholera would be instantly diagnosed by him, he would be isolated and the alleged cholera would be reported up to the most senior Japanese; the ultimate consequences could be disastrous for him and his friends.

The vomiting ended at about nine o'clock at night, perhaps some ten hours after it had started. But the headache lasted a little longer. Then, physically spent, he slept until rudely awakened the next morning. The Sergeant Major was understanding – Ian's friends having explained the background to him – but he insisted that he clean up the smelly mess immediately. His friends left him to that chore, probably thinking they had already been put to enough trouble by him the previous day and night.

Before joining the Amoebic Battalion, Oliver had been caught by the camp police whilst in the act of re-entering the camp one night after a purchasing foray. He was then held in their guardroom for three days and was stripped of all his personal possessions other than essentials like mess tin, water bottle, spoon and blankets. The camp police force, a group of big and tough POWs, was a Japanese institution formed to reduce the burden of Japanese perimeter patrols; the head of the force was a British officer.

Oliver had been bitter about the incident. But when he learned from his friends in the Battalion about excursions at night to bring in drugs, he understood that so long as the Japanese trusted the camp police to prevent perimeter breaches, it was easier to come and go. And if it was deemed necessary for the camp police to deter perimeter breaches by all and sundry so as to make it safer to operate mercy missions, then their harsh treatment of miscreants was understood. But they were still unloved.

On the eve of the new year there was a camp concert, probably the first in Chungkai. It was a good and varied performance by a variety of talented artists, including Bobby Spong, a female impersonator. The camp was in desperate need of being cheered up since deaths were still a daily occurrence and there were still hundreds of grievously sick men. A rousing song, written by a POW and sung by the entire audience at the end of the performance, lifted the men quite a bit. The words were assertive and positive. They did not express hopes or wishes or longings; so far as the men were concerned the words they sang stated what would happen clearly, simply and certainly. The bold statement that 'Ships will meet us at Rangoon, We will see Southampton soon' would surely be remembered by all of them for the rest of their lives. And would any be able to forget the earlier line explaining that 'They can stick the railway up the Three Pagoda Pass'? They had already been POWs for twenty-two and a half months – it was wise of them not to contemplate how much longer their ordeal was to last. Ian reminded himself that everyone should be glad they had been there that long, because they were now that much closer to freedom – but those twenty-two and a half months had cost many precious lives and a great deal of pain and suffering, so he could be forgiven if he sometimes forgot to be glad that so much time had passed.

During the weeks of January 1944, and in the days preceding 15 February which was the second anniversary of the surrender, Ian, and probably many others, went through a depressing time. On occasions his mind dwelt upon the darkness, cruelty and wickedness of the evil Japanese empire. In this state he could not easily understand how men flying in planes just a few thousand yards away were free in a bright and decent world. He was much troubled because he had seen enough of Japanese occupation in Singapore and Thailand to know that their empire was indeed dark and evil, not just for their enemies opposed to them in war, but for the Asian masses in the occupied countries too. He felt as though they were almost in a separate world where horrendous evil and darkness persisted and might be difficult to overcome.

On occasions he escaped from the depressive moods by wilful dreaming, perhaps mildly hallucinating, that he could fly, just as birds do but with extended arms instead of wings. In his dream he circled high above the camp tormenting and mocking the Japanese below, before heading off west to join the Allied forces in Burma. He was glad when 15 February was past and was never again overcome by such a miserable mood.

Oliver Hartley continued with his occasional excursions to the Thai village but never became involved in anything other than small individual purchases. In Chungkai, and probably in all other camps in Thailand, there never was any black-market importation on the scale which had existed in Singapore's River Valley Road camp. Apart from noble efforts to bring in medicines, no POW was known to shop for more than his own personal consumption. The likely reason for such constraint was that the Japanese regime in Thailand had shown itself to be extremely harsh when meting out punishment to defaulters.

There was a cooler in Chungkai, a bamboo cage with the dimensions of a five-foot cube which was exposed to the full ferocity of the sun. The prisoner would have to spend two days, or longer, sitting cross-legged during his entire period there; if he was lucky he would be let out twice a day on the end of rope for visits to the latrine; food would be supplied through the bars of his cage, sometimes in a container, sometimes tipped on the earth floor; whenever the guard changed the patrol would pass the cooler and the prisoner would be slapped, if that had been prescribed as part of his punishment. And in Chungkai the cooler was more usually occupied than unoccupied because it was used for offences which could not be deemed serious by any reasonable standard. Since it was strategically placed for viewing by the rest of the camp, it might have been a deterrent to men contemplating 'crimes'. Perhaps it was, but thankfully it did not deter them all.

Oliver's presence in the hut was good for the men who knew him. He strayed far and wide within the camp, but his friends knew that he was probably not in literal breach of the rule that those with amoebic dysentery must not wander around. He always had his ear to the ground, knew how to find his way about and was a ready source of generally reliable information which was often cheerful, and certainly never boring to men starved of news about anything at all.

The obtaining of tobacco had never been a serious problem in Thailand; the problem had always been how to smoke it in the absence of paper for making cigarettes. Letters from home were few and far between and, but for a few early exceptions, were only postcards; true, they could be soaked and then parted into three layers of thick paper, but not many cigarettes could be made from those infrequent cards. Dictionaries and bibles had been smoked to extinction during the first weeks in Thailand because their pages were so suited for cigarette making; the thicker paper of the pages of ordinary books had preserved the books for only a little longer but inevitably they, too, were rolled into extinction during those early days.

In Chungkai, the Thai canteen stocked manufactured Thai cigarettes, tobacco and cigarette papers of a reasonable quality. The cigarettes were too expensive for POWs, but tobacco and the rolling paper, in two qualities, was affordable. A Dutch POW designed a simple machine, using two blocks of wood and a small piece of light canvas, which was easy to use to produce well made cigarettes. He experimented with the tobacco, learnt by trial and error how to 'cure' the tobacco by adequate rinsing and drying, and then set himself up in the business of making and selling cigarettes of a quality nearly as good as that of the Thai manufactured ones. Soon he set up a factory, gave his cigarettes a brand name and employed some men to make them, and others to hawk them around; they were a great success, even though affordable to only a minority in camp. He was the only baron in the camp.

A disturbing story circulated the camp. It concerned a British POW who acquired empty quinine bottles which had been discarded by the Japanese. He filled them with tapioca flour and sealed the corks to the bottles by heating and reshaping remnants of the original wax seals. Each bottle then resembled an unopened bottle of quinine as supplied to the Japanese army, complete with Japanese label. Subsequently he went out at night and sold, or traded, a bottle on each occasion. Inevitably, after just a few weeks of the shameful operation, the Thai villagers discovered they were being cheated. On his next visit the man was stabbed; the Thais could have killed him, but chose only to wound, and he returned with the knife still in his back. The authenticity of the story was not doubted.

News of any kind was difficult to get in the camps in Thailand. News of the course of the war was rare indeed, and even when such news was circulated it was impossible for the men to know if it was genuine or simply a rumour started up by some bored or cranky individual. And even when there was cause to believe that the news had a genuine basis, how could anyone know that the facts had not been distorted during the passage of the rumours from one camp to the next. And the complexity of possibilities did not end there, because any responsible person disseminating news always corrupted it so that were the story to reach the Japanese they would not be able to detect from it that there must be a radio in camp. All knew that the penalty for being caught with a radio – or for even just listening to one – was probably execution. So the men believed that the chances of there being a secret radio in camp were indeed minimal.

From the earliest days in Singapore outrageous rumours had circulated and been believed initially, but when disproved by time those who had been fooled were left with reduced morale. The stage had long since been set for general disbelief of any item of war news. Anyone repeating such news given to him was in danger of being brushed off, or even ridiculed and told he must be an incredible idiot for even thinking that the news might be genuine. Spontaneous irritation against anyone trying to pass on something he overheard, or was told, was not uncommon even when he prefaced the item with the overworked phrase, 'I've just heard some borehole news.' Most men had reached the stage where they instinctively disbelieved any item of news unless told to them first hand by a senior officer, and there was no chance of that happening to the men, or even to junior officers, in those camps. They were a disillusioned, cynical lot.

There had been persistent stories to the effect that Sicily had been invaded, and shortly afterwards that the Allies were fighting on the Italian mainland. 'If only that were true. If only there was some evidence that the news was true,' was the initial reaction of most. But the stories persisted and many reacted by wondering how significant the news was, even if true. How well or badly were things going? Was the enemy being driven back? Or was it slow progress, even stalemate? The persistence of the rumours, and their gradual development, led to the stories being accepted as being basically true – but how significant was it all? As days went by most men accepted the truth of the rumours that the invasion of Italy was succeeding, but though cheered, many felt tense and strained with worry lest there be any serious setback. And this was especially so if fresh news of further advances was not forthcoming regularly. The effects on the men of being denied radio or printed news during their captivity cannot be overstated – even a hungry undernourished man would certainly have chosen a radio update of war news rather than a good square meal if he was given the choice.

Whoever masterminded the steady dripping of the news to the men did a good job – just a little at a time, so that there was always progress to report. Before very long the men's confidence in the news, and in the success of the campaign, was established. This happy state of affairs continued progressively.

The railway had been more or less completed. The Japanese informed the camp that many men were to be sent to Japan. Only the fittest were chosen and each was issued with a pair of blue cotton shorts, a trilby, white socks and canvas shoes. There was

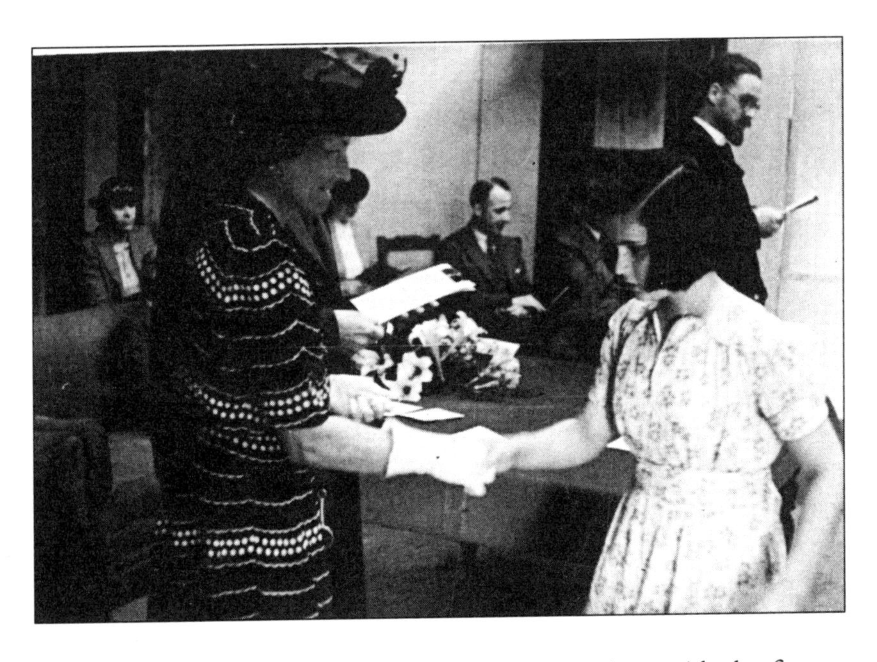

Photograph received by Ian from his evacuee sister with the first batch of letters he received in late 1943.

much activity and excitement. The men chosen to go were generally excited by the prospect and most in camp were of the opinion that conditions in POW camps in Japan had to be better than those in Thailand, or elsewhere in the Japanese empire. Their reasoning was that the Japanese nation was too civilised to mistreat so badly their prisoners, and that the Japanese government would not tolerate such abysmal treatment of POWs by their army, if they knew about it. Was not the issue of new clothing to those chosen to go, and the fact that only the fittest were chosen, an indication that the Japanese army in Thailand wished to conceal from their government the conditions in their POW camps?

However, many were less certain that conditions in Japan would be significantly better. Then there was also the journey there to think about. All had experienced the four day rail journey from Singapore to Thailand, and none was stupid enough to assume that travel in the overcrowded holds of small Japanese ships would be anything other than at least ten times worse. After the initial excitement about the prospect of being sent to Japan had died down, in the cool light of day it seemed to most that those men in the Japan party who still genuinely looked forward to the move must surely have had a memory lapse. Or perhaps they had a greater sense of adventure than was good for them. In a matter of days the men marched out of the camp to the railway *en route* for Singapore and Japan.

Their departure was only the start of a mass exodus of POWs from Chungkai. A few small working parties were sent upriver to maintain the bridges and stretches of the railway. A substantial proportion of the remainder, including sick, were to be sent to base camps down-river. The dispersal of the men to down-river camps depended upon the administrative groups to which the individuals belonged when first sent to Thailand to build the railroad. This would result in friends being parted – possibly never to meet again. For example, Oliver Hartley was destined for Nakhon Patom which lay between Ban Pong and Bangkok; Ian, in Group 4, was destined for Tamuang which was located between Kanchanaburi and Ban Pong.

In the middle of May 1944 Ian, with others from the Amoebic Battalion, left by barge for Tamuang. At that time records relating to Group 2 personnel, which had been centralised in Chungkai, showed that of the original 7200 British POWs in the group, some 1700 had already died in Chungkai and in other camps. But all knew that many more would die because hundreds were still grievously ill.

The barge journey was silent, uneventful and could even have been tranquil if men had no memories. But memories they certainly did have. Not much was said on the barges because the pain, cruelty, sickness, anguish, misery, trauma and sadness which had been their lot since leaving Singapore twenty months earlier was common to them all, and memories which were now inevitably at the forefront, hurt. There was nothing to be said which would help any of them. The men, though densely packed together on the barge, were each alone and separate in their thoughts. And that was how those men needed to be at that time.

CHAPTER 5

Tamuang

IT WAS EVENING, merely an hour or so before dusk, when the barges pulled in to the river bank beside the small jetty for the men to disembark. A wide path from the riverside led to the main part of the camp where they were met and guided to a hut where they would spend the night. Captain Pavillard, the MO who had been at Wampo when Ian and six others with dysentery were sent to Chungkai about fifteen months earlier, greeted them. It was an excited greeting – not a medical inspection, that would follow the next morning. He remembered Ian; it was impressive that the MO who must have attended hundreds in the last fifteen months still remembered them after all that time; he asked if he had been right in his diagnosis of amoebic dysentery.

Since Captain Pavillard was in this camp, Ian thought his brother Ron might also be there, so he set out to enquire. He spotted Frank Goodall, his platoon sergeant, talking to another platoon member, both of whom had been at Wampo; they were looking out for familiar faces among the new arrivals. Both were surprised by him, and took a second or so to realise who he was, or so it seemed at first. Ian came straight to the point. 'Where's Ron?' he asked. After a little hesitation Goodall said, 'We left him at Tonchan, didn't we?' Fred Barretto was quick to agree. They said no more about Ron; there was no mention of how he had fared, how fit he was when they last saw him, why he had been left behind. Ian's conclusion that Ron had died and they had not worked out how to tell him was perhaps inevitable from a young man in the circumstances of that emotional day. He did not tell them of the conclusion he had jumped to. Neither did he even suspect that the initial silence and confusion of the two had been due to their surprise when they recognised him – they had heard some weeks earlier that he had died of amoebic dysentery. Ian left them quickly and returned to his hut in silence.

By the next morning Ian knew he had to cheer up and take things in his stride, and he gradually did so. The newcomers from the former Amoebic Battalion were moved into the hospital, where Captain Pavillard visited and checked on each of them. The day was then spent seeking out former acquaintances, and generally relaxing. The relaxing helped Ian quite a bit; he decided that in the evening when the workers were back in camp he would visit Frank Goodall and others from Wampo, and get some firm answers about Ron, because it had dawned on him he might possibly have jumped to a wrong conclusion the previous evening.

His visit in the evening to see his platoon friends from Wampo was a joyful one for him. Ron had been in excellent health when last seen at Tonchan camp just a few weeks earlier, and he had volunteered to stay with a small maintenance party; it was likely the job they were on would soon end, so probably he would arrive in Tamuang before very long. Ian did not come clean and tell them of the mistake he had made the previous evening, and neither did they own up to him that they had believed him to have died weeks earlier.

Two mornings later Ian, together with Bill Dobbs, Grahame Gardiner and others, was whiling away the time after the MO's round, when on the path leading to the end entrance of the hut, Ron appeared. He was striding purposefully, erect, bulging with muscles Ian had not seen before, and seemingly very fit. Ian met him at the entrance and took him back to meet his friends, whom Ron knew only slightly. Ron told him he had arrived in Tamuang about an hour earlier and was told that his brother was alive and where he was. He, and their friends, had been told weeks earlier that Ian had died of amoebic dysentery – they knew now that it was a case of mistaken identity and that it was, in fact, Mexican Mitch who had died. Ian did not tell Ron, or anyone else, of the wrong conclusion he had jumped to.

Ron could not dally; he had been allowed to break off to visit his brother, but had to return urgently to be assimilated into the hut, hopefully in a location near his friends.

Ian visited him in the evening and heard how Ron had fared during the 'Speedo'. He had cerebral malaria and nearly died from it; he still had frequent bouts of malaria but his system had learned to cope and the attacks were no longer serious; he had been nearly strangled by a drunken Japanese. Whilst acutely ill with cerebral malaria, Melville Hartley had seen him in a hospital – Melville had been with 'F' Force, which with 'H' Force, had comprised 10,000 men who had been sent from Singapore during the height of the 'Speedo', and within a matter of weeks some 6,000 of them had died. He had since been returned to Singapore with the remnants of the original 10,000.

Ian listened to the horrendous events which had occurred to Ron and his friends, shaking his head, not in disbelief but in dismay that all that had happened. He had heard it all before in Chungkai, but it was still compulsive listening when related by people he knew so well – and it was still shocking to him. He did not tell them much about Chungkai, only that he was one of the fortunates to receive emetine, and that Oliver Hartley was there and was OK.

Ian realised how very unfit he was when he compared himself with Ron and others he had been with at River Valley Road camp and during the earliest days at Wampo. Ron and his friends suggested he should stay in hospital for as long as possible; work each day was still heavy and this big base camp contained most of the notorious Japanese guards who had beaten and killed in railway camps. Were he to be in a working party under one of them, he would be in dire trouble unless he really was fit enough to perform heavy work. Ian was anxious to get out among his friends and become fit so he volunteered to assist a small working party building an operating theatre. The Japanese had permitted a small workforce for the project – which worked without Japanese supervision – and had also provided some bamboo and atap. The building had been completed but beds and operating tables had yet to be made, and there was no more bamboo left. Ian was working under the instructions of a corporal and volunteered to 'scrounge' some suitable bamboo; the corporal told him to be careful. Nearby were other working groups erecting structures for the Japanese, each group under the control of a guard. Some seventy yards away from the operating theatre there was a group whose guard was not present, so Ian took advantage of the absence, selected lengths of bamboo from the pile there and sawed them into seven-foot lengths. He finished sawing, tied the lengths into a bundle and was about to depart when the POW sergeant leading the working group asked what the hell he was doing. Ian explained. The sergeant was alarmed and told him the guard in charge of the party was the Black Prince and he had personally chosen the straightest and best bamboos for the construction of a guardroom. He told Ian to take the bamboo away quickly and he would do what he could to mislead the Black Prince.

Ian returned to the operating theatre with the bamboo and was complimented by the corporal on his successful expedition – until told how he got the bamboo, and from whom. The Black Prince was a vicious guard who had beaten several men to death during the railway construction so the two men watched his return to his working party in fearful anticipation. The corporal told Ian that if the guard challenged them he was to keep quiet and leave the talking to him. They watched him return and his reaction when he surveyed the off-cuts and realised his selected bamboo had mostly gone. The POW sergeant replied to his screams by vaguely pointing in the direction of other working groups, including the operating theatre. The Black Prince sawed a bamboo into a four-foot length and strode out towards the operating theatre. The corporal and Ian were fearful of the consequences of the seemingly inevitable confrontation, and Ian was reminded that the corporal should be left to do all the denials.

Halfway to the operating theatre the guard altered direction and made for another Japanese-led working group about fifty yards away. As soon as he arrived there he exchanged angry words with the guard in charge of that party, and obviously accused him of the theft of the bamboo. That guard then armed himself with a bamboo club and both men set about each other in violent combat. Some two hundred POWs surrounded them at a discreet distance, and with even more discreet silence, as they first of all aimed and warded off club blows, then lost their clubs and punched and wrestled each other to the ground. A Japanese sergeant, seeing the commotion from a distance, rushed over and ordered the men apart. He slapped them both.

Ian and the corporal knew they had had a narrow and fortunate escape. Ian was brought to his senses – he had exposed himself to serious risks in Singapore's River Valley Road camp by taking chances with his captors and had promised himself he would not do it again. Yet he had thoughtlessly taken a risk, with fearful consequences if he was caught, and he would have been caught if the Black Prince had returned just five minutes earlier. He knew the months in Chungkai where he had not been troubled by the attention of individual guards had blunted his awareness of the need for caution, and he resolved to be more careful; especially because there were more murderous guards like the Black Prince in Tamuang.

The nicknames by which many guards had become known throughout the railway camps, were all very logical. The Prince was a guard who claimed to be distantly related to the Japanese royal family; the Black Prince was so named because he was dark skinned and his true name sounded the same as that of the Prince; the Silver Bullet had a silver bullet mascot hanging from his waist; the Kanu Kid was an officer who had been commandant at Kanu Camp – he swaggered around in tight fitting, low hipped, American styled trousers, padded shoulders and a pistol adorning each hip – whose mother, it was said, had probably been impressed by a cowboy; the Mad Mongrel was liable to pick up a bamboo and go berserk with it – hitting all within reach – for no obvious reason; Holy Joe was a Christian who hardly mixed with his fellow guards and who, it was said, took off his boots before kicking; the Works Master was in charge of apportioning labour and overseeing the rate of progress of jobs; Pig's Vomit was a diseased guard whose behaviour and talk were so disgusting that his nickname was well deserved. There were others, too, but none so colourful or obnoxious as these. Some of the guards knew their nicknames and were proud of them – even Pig's Vomit, who was led to believe his name meant 'Japanese gentleman number one', was boastful and announced it to the men whenever he was sent to a new camp.

Tamuang camp was located in an area where the terrain was entirely clay. The Japanese had agreed to a request that men be allowed to build a kiln in which to bake bricks which they wished to make, to enable an oven to be built for the cookhouse. The small kiln, which was built mostly submerged below ground level, was a success and the bricks produced were of a reasonable quality; the cookhouse was soon equipped with an oven in which to bake

SERVICE DE PRISONNIERS DE GUERRE.

FROM MOTHER.

MRS A. O. MITCHELL,
L.M.R.M. SCHOOL,
LOVEDALE,
NILGIRIS,
S. INDIA.

TO.
No. 13893,
PTE. I. H. MITCHELL
BRITISH PRISONER OF WAR
4(1) P.O.W. CAMP,
THAILAND

PASSED
DHP/9

LOVEDALE
26 FEB 44

C/O PRISONER OF WAR
INFORMATION BUREAU
TOKYO.

DHP/135

IAN DARLING,
DELIGHTED RECEIVE YOUR THIRD CARD. AWAITING FROM THREE OTHERS.
HOPE ALL WELL WITH YOU.
BOTH WELL. JEAN DOING WELL COMMERCIAL MADRAS. QUITE GROWN UP.
THINKING ALL CONTINUALLY.
FONDEST LOVE & KISSES,
Mum.

Card from Ian's mother

balls of boiled rice until they had a brown crust, when they could be dubbed 'bread cobs'. The alleged bread cobs, which were a change from dollops of hopeless stodgy rice, were almost a luxury, in appearance, anyway; the oven was large enough to bake, at one pass, sufficient for about a quarter of the men in camp. Since the additional labour required to make these bakes was normally unavailable, they became a luxury available only on special days.

The success of the brick kiln and cookhouse oven led to the construction of a large sterilisation oven in which the men's clothes and blankets could be sterilised, in a massive effort to eliminate the lice which lived and multiplied in clothing and blankets. In a well planned operation, all the clothing and blankets belonging to the men in groups of huts, were labelled and placed in the steriliser for twenty-four hours before being returned to the men; then it was the turn of the clothing and blankets in the next group of huts to be dealt with, and this continued until all had had attention.

The sterilisation programme was successful only to a limited extent. It seemed that lice were all killed but some eggs, at least, survived; furthermore, men were continually returning to Tamuang from other working camps, and brought with them breeding stocks of lice. Thus, although the louse population was dramatically reduced by the sterilisation programme, it was only a matter of weeks before they regained their numbers and continued to plague the men, just as bugs and mosquitoes did.

The ability of the men to make bricks of a reasonable quality was a fact not lost on the camp commandant. He ordered the construction of three large brick kilns within the camp perimeter, so that he could sell bricks to Thai merchants. But first a new house would be built for him, a traditional Japanese house, but on brick pillars to keep it about five feet above the ground. He set aside a labour force of twenty-five men and maintained a permanent interest in his private venture.

The commandant had hand-picked the guards who would have overall control of the men working on the enterprise, and of course had also ordered that the POW mastermind who had designed the original kiln and overseen its operation had a free hand in design, construction and operation. Brick quality was improved upon, and commercial potential in Kanchanaburi was never doubted. The commandant's house was soon built; all bricks produced subsequently were sold to Thais, which provided the commandant with a very nice little earner for his personal benefit.

The men who had charge of the kilns were there on a permanent basis. Those who moulded the bricks and stacked them in the sun for three days to dry, prior to being placed in the kilns, were casual workers whom the guard took for this work after roll-call each morning. He unfailingly chose the first twenty men on parade, and since work at the brickyard was thought to be preferable, and safer, than other jobs because the guard was not a notorious murderer, there was keen competition to be in the brickyard party. Consequently, men eager to be taken for the brickyard job paraded for roll-call earlier and earlier each day.

Ian had been discharged from hospital. On his first days back as a worker he had not competed for brickyard work and usually ended up in a working party destined for a day's work in Kanchanaburi. They were conveyed there in an open lorry, standing and holding on to one another, because their lives depended on it in that lurching, swaying vehicle. Halfway to Kanchanaburi was a camp of Indian labourers, men and women and some children too, who had survived the railway construction. They seemed wretched, in a poor physical state, and watched the lorry go by each day seemingly without any emotion or interest; the men in the lorry always felt real sorrow that such uninvolved, poor and helpless people had been brought up from the plantations of Malaya to suffer the horrors they endured on the railway project. Why the Japanese kept them in Thailand rather than return them to their homes in Malaya was not a mystery – clearly the Japanese did not wish people to take back to Malaya the truth about what had been done to them, how 140,000 out of 200,000 Indian labourers had died within a few weeks of their arrival in the jungle to build a railway. That would hardly be good propaganda for the Greater East Asia Co-Prosperity Sphere, which was what the Japanese called the territories they had occupied and enslaved.

In Kanchanaburi the working party mostly loaded or unloaded trucks or barges; the work was heavy, as Ian found to his cost. He soon realised that the muscles in his torso were reasonably strong, but his hands and feet were weak. Lifting and carrying heavy sacks of rice seemed to tax him a great deal more than others, and it seemed that a guard was permanently scolding him. After a few days of such work he decided he should, in future, try to get into the brickyard working party even if it was necessary to turn up for roll-call very early each morning.

So it was that Ian joined the other early birds and took up his position in roll-call parade some forty minutes prior to each morning's roll-call, and for the rest of his time in Tamuang he worked at the brickyard. Initially he was a 'supplier' : he and three others dug clay and carried it on bamboo stretchers to the 'puddlers'. The puddlers added water to the clay and puddled the mixture with their feet until it was a suitable consistency for the nearby 'moulders'. The moulders stood in a three foot deep trench so that the ground in front of them was their workbench; each slapped clay into his wooden frame which had been placed on a board and dusted with brick dust, then, using a thin wire which was held taut by a bamboo bow, the surplus clay would be cut off the top. The moulded brick would then be carried off for drying in the sun. After three days in the sun, the bricks were ready for baking in the kiln for five days. And the smug look of satisfaction on the commandant's face when he surveyed his infallible money spinner each day, was understandable.

The height of Ian's working career in Tamuang was reached when he graduated from 'supplying' to 'puddling' and then to 'moulding'. In one context, at least, it could be said that life was simple in those days!

At least one man in Tamuang was going through a mental breakdown. His mental state had gone unnoticed until he packed his haversack, combed his hair and declared that he had had enough of Thailand and was going home. He was not taken seriously until he had marched up to the sentry at the gate, given him a smart salute and asked for the gate to be opened. The sentry had let him out, then when the man had taken several strides towards Ban Pong – which was many miles away – the not so bright sentry had realised his error and run after him to bring the poor fellow back to camp.

It was easy enough for the MO to convince the Japanese that the man was out of his mind. But then the MO had the more difficult task of persuading the Japanese that it would be kinder to look after the fellow than to shoot him – because that was the treatment the Japanese favoured. They wanted to shoot him, not as a punishment, but simply to end his madness, just as a horse with a badly broken leg would be put down.

Ultimately the commandant agreed that he need not be shot. Instead, he would wear a wooden badge on which his insanity was proclaimed in Japanese characters. And he also had to be contained securely in a bamboo cage in a camp hospital hut. Fortunately for the man he did not seem to mind very much, but care was still needed because he seemed to be always trying to trick someone into releasing him. The fear was that were he to try to go home again he would be executed.

In June 1944, on a rest day, a Japanese medical team arrived unannounced in Tamuang camp. It included one British person, X, who had been at school with Ian, but who being older had left school to join the Royal Army Medical Corps before the outbreak of the Japanese war. And here he was in Tamuang, a civilian in spotless white clothes, unescorted and walking across the empty parade ground. Ian saw him and each recognised the other instantly. Ian set out to cross the parade ground aiming to pass him, and X altered the direction of his walk so that they would pass one another. Since talking to civilians was a serious offence, both for POW and civilian, they did not look at each other or alter their walking speed as they passed a few feet apart, but X spoke. He said, 'We have invaded France successfully. Good progress.'

X's news was a confirmation of rumours which were being whispered around, and whose authenticity Ian had wanted to believe, but dared not. Now he had no further cause for doubt. The next day Ian and many others were kept in their huts for the Japanese medical team to take blood samples. X and one Japanese took samples from the men in Ian's hut, and it was X who pricked Ian's ear for a drop of blood – their eyes met – but neither dared speak because of the nearby presence of the Japanese medic, whom Ian observed keeping a close eye on X.

No one seemed to know the objective of that medical team. For Ian, the matter was more puzzling. He had not seen or heard of X in any POW camp in Singapore or Thailand until then. He wondered if the Japanese knew he was a British serviceman, and how it was that he was a civilian in Japanese employment. Ian did not suppose then, or ever, that X was a collaborator and never doubted then, or ever, that he was always a loyal Briton. He was glad they met and that X had delivered such good news.

One POW in Tamuang had a better job than most. Each day, escorted by a guard, he drove a lorry to Ban Pong to collect rations. Usually the days were uneventful, but on one occasion he returned to Tamuang with quite a story. On the way to Tamuang he had stopped, as usual, at a village for the guard to visit a Thai coffee house, which was also frequented by other Japanese soldiers. At these stops the POW always remained in the lorry and patiently awaited the return of the guard. On this day a Thai approached the POW and offered to buy the rifle which the guard had left on the passenger seat. They haggled about the price and then did their deal, the Thai disappearing with the rifle well before the guard returned. In due course the guard came back and they drove off on their final leg to Tamuang. Halfway home the rifle was missed and the guard asked the POW, 'My gun, where?' When told by the POW that the guard had taken it into the coffee shop, the Japanese demanded an about turn and a speedo back to the coffee shop. At the coffee shop the guard dashed in, emerged with a rifle after a few minutes, ran to the lorry and demanded a speedo back to camp. As they approached Tamuang he told the POW he could not find his own rifle so had picked up one belonging to another soldier. He gave the POW a packet of cigarettes for his speedo driving.

In about the middle of July hundreds of Japanese soldiers were seen marching, or rather straggling, on the road outside camp, which led from Ban Pong to Kanchanaburi. All seemed to be in a state of near exhaustion. The scene reminded Ian of his tribulations on the first two days of his march on the same road from Ban Pong to Kanchanaburi nearly two years earlier. He knew he should not feel sorry for them, but it was difficult not to understand the state they were in.

The guards in camp had become more edgy of late, more impatient, more hasty in their reactions, and seemed to have lost some of their previous unchallenged confidence. The commandant ordered that the men must not collect in groups of more than four to converse. Larger groups, whether at roll call or work or Sunday service etc., were not allowed to converse unless a guard was present. One day Ian was in a group of four when the Silver Bullet walked past; three of the group noticed him and saluted, as was the requirement. But the fourth, Ivan Newman, had his back to the guard and was slow to turn about and salute – he would have been quicker had he known the identity of the guard his friends were saluting – so the Silver Bullet beat him up. After the event the three sought to sympathise with Ivan, but he preferred to dismiss the incident, saying, 'I've always known he was jealous of my moustache; did you notice his patchy growth?'

One guard, an unpopular fellow with the men because he was always unpleasant and threatening, had pleased the commandant by his efforts to drive the men harder, and had become too bossy and arrogant for his own good. He answered back to a Japanese sergeant who maintained his supremacy by killing him with a single blow to the back of his neck with a crowbar. The next morning, at roll call, the commandant announced the death: 'Mr Eu-kee is dead. Today all men rest and mourn for a good soldier.' It was an unexpected holiday for the men who were experienced enough at being POWs to enjoy the rest during the day without any display of good cheer until the evening, when they had an impromptu concert. The commandant halted the concert, saying that it was not decent to be joyful on a day of mourning.

In August 1944 a major in the IJA addressed the entire camp. He spoke with the aid of his interpreter who translated each sentence as it was spoken. Armed guards, with bayonets fixed, were spaced between the rows of men, which indicated that all should be attentive and none should offend the major by any discourtesy whatever. There was venom, spite and hate in his words and bearing; his speech was long, with many warnings, threats and boasts. The gist of his unsolicited message was that the war would last one hundred years, the men would never see their families again, they would die in the service of the Emperor in one of the new Japanese territories or, if truly fortunate, in Japan itself. If they died working hard they would only partly have atoned for the evils of the Western nations against the Japanese nation, yet because they would then have died for the Emperor they would go to paradise. Were they to die of illness or because they had not worked hard enough, or because they were disobedient or for any other unworthy reason, then their souls would be deprived of paradise, because that was decreed by Bushido. He said the men would have new opportunities to do major construction work since much construction was required in the territories which the colonial powers had neglected; many more railways, roads and bridges had to be built. He urged the men to face up to the realistic situation which was that their armies had forsaken them, and it was understandable that those armies were concerned only with saving their own skins in the face of superior Japanese armies, particularly because Western people lacked honour in battle and did not have the spirit, courage and wisdom of Bushido to guide them.

At the end the men were dismissed from the parade. The speech had a serious effect on the men, at first. They returned to their huts in silence and with some sense of foreboding. The wiser heads among the men quickly pointed to the likelihood that the Japanese were taking a beating somewhere, or that they recognised that Germany was well on the way to being defeated and then their turn to face the full might of the Allies would surely follow. They thought the speech was from a fanatic who was too furious with the turn of events to recognise that Japan was doomed.

But despite the wisdom of the wiser heads, the mood of the men became quieter and less optimistic than it had been. Mood swings were frequent in those camps, which were so cut off from the outside world, because the men themselves never heard news first hand and had suffered so much trauma in the previous two and a half years.

To the rescue came Padre Harry Thorpe. He was a driver in the Australian Army, having declined a commission which was offered to him to become a chaplain in the Australian forces. He had preferred to be near and with the men whom he would regard as his flock – to share their problems so that he could understand better. He had already become a legend in POW camps, and it was known that he was the well intentioned source of many strategic and optimistic rumours whenever dismal events or foreboding depressed the spirit of men in the camps. The padre rose to the occasion wonderfully. He already knew that no one any longer doubted that the landing in Europe had occurred and been successful, so he chose a hymn for the approaching Sunday service and caused his notices advertising the hymn and service to be posted in prominent places. The leading words of the hymn appeared on notices, not just the hymn number and name:

> 'The strife is o'er, the battle done
> Now is the victor's triumph won.'

The hymn was chosen to convey that the Allies were doing magnificently in France, and that the European war was well on its way towards the defeat of Germany. It was only August 1944 and it was not known whether he personally started the rumours about the soon to be defeated Germany, or whether his brilliant choice of that Easter hymn, so late in the year, led others to believe the hymn was chosen to inform the camp of good news. Very few in Tamuang failed to attend that Sunday service and the Japanese guard, whose presence at services was a stipulated IJA requirement, must have wondered what was so special about that Sunday because the attendance was so great and the singing so enthusiastic. Certainly Harry Thorpe had lifted the spirits in Tamuang to heights above those existing before the Japanese major's address.

Whenever war news was leaked to the men it was always good positive stuff which lifted spirits – no one ever reported war news which was not good, and strangely enough that phenomenon was not noticed. It was, perhaps, that the men were like ostriches and had blotted out any thought of adverse military events afflicting the Allies. But, more than likely, they felt that possibly enough time had passed for the Allies to arm and organise a military effort which was invincible. They were troubled by a persistent foreboding that they would be massacred before the end of hostilities, rather than that hostilities would drag on and on. For it seemed to them that such an end would be proclaimed by the Japanese to be in keeping with the spirit of Bushido.

Daily a working party at Tamuang railway 'station' loaded supplies on to trains bound for Burma. No one had any doubt the supplies were for the Japanese forces. That the supplies were sometimes clearly labelled as being Red Cross parcels for prisoners of war made no difference – such parcels had been loaded on trains for a long time and none had ever been distributed to the men in Thailand. The men knew the contents of those parcels were bound to end up in the mouths of Japanese soldiers in Burma. The Japanese obviously thought it fair game to take whatever they wanted – they had behaved in that way to the POWs ever since the men were first captured and were stripped of their valuables such as watches, rings and fountain pens.

So it was not surprising that the POWs deemed all Japanese goods, whether in a warehouse, on a lorry, train or barge, or even in the personal possession of Japanese soldiers, to be fair game which should be stolen for POW consumption, or destroyed or damaged – that had become a POW sport since the earliest days of captivity. Men who successfully scored in that sport felt good about their achievement – it promoted their macho – and if the event involved making monkeys of Japanese, then the achievement was all the more commendable and was often recalled in POW camp lore.

The working party at Tamuang station was lectured by a guard one morning immediately before their work started. His lecture concerned the fact that he knew 'all English Australia soldier bruddy great thief'. With words and actions he then explained – more or less accurately – how they operated their thieving at that job. He was in his element and in triumphant mood. He said, 'All soldier watch me,' and then picked up a parcel, looked around furtively and then deliberately dropped the parcel on the concrete floor, intending the parcel to break open. But it did not break so he indicated that the men should assume it had broken and the contents had fallen out . . . He then went through the motions of picking up the contents and placing them carefully on a work-table, demonstrating the action by placing his cigarette lighter and a packet of cigarettes on the table. He then moved a few feet away from the table, went through the act of looking around furtively before returning to the table and snatching the lighter and cigarettes to hide them under the hat he was wearing. His act was a little spoilt because his snatch had been inaccurate and he had missed both items. But it did not matter to him because he knew he had made his point, and triumphantly strode up and down the line of men telling them that the game was up because 'Japanese soldier very intelligent'. And he went back to the table where he discovered that his lighter was there, but not his cigarettes.

He raged and threatened the men who were still lined up. He searched each man thoroughly – that was easy because boots, hat and jap-happy were all that the men wore – but the packet of cigarettes was not found. The straight-faced men looked hurt and confused and told the guard over and over again that he placed the cigarettes under his cap; one man took a chance and complimented the guard on a good magician's trick which they could not fathom.

The guard gave up. He was confused and in any case the train was waiting to be loaded. So the men started work, still with the most puzzled look they could muster. They did not discuss how one of them had deftly grabbed the cigarettes and hurled them into the jungle behind him whilst the guard was in the middle of his triumphant, but amateurish act.

Tamuang was a base camp from which working parties would be drawn and sent out for the day on one-off jobs, or on a regular daily basis or even for weeks or months at a time. Typically, parties were sent upriver on railway repair jobs. More and more working parties were sent away for variable lengths of time and it was clear that the camp was not a haven of rest just because it was a base camp. There seemed to be a general manpower shortage in the camp because, from time to time, men were called upon for additional work after their normal working day had finished. For a brief period they were required to unload sacks of rice from barges and carry them to a large storehouse some four hundred yards or so from the river. Each sack weighed seventy-five kilos – which was no mean weight to carry for any but the fittest – and would be lifted on to the shoulders of the men whose only concern then was to stagger to the storehouse as best they could, and with as much speed as possible so that they could be unburdened quickly. Were any man to drop his sack before the journey was completed there would not be anyone to replace it on his shoulders, and the watching guards would be a threat. Sometimes the men were required to do two such loads. Thus it was that Ian learned that his legs, especially his ankles and feet, were still weak. On those trips his stagger to the storehouse was a great deal more wobbly than that of the others. He came to accept the inevitability that he would not return to his former fitness until the war was over and he was rebuilt by proper nourishment.

The Japanese announced that Red Cross parcels had arrived for the men in the camp and would soon be handed over for distribution. The label on each parcel indicated that it was a regular monthly parcel for one man. But there were not enough parcels for one per person – there were enough only for the share out to be two parcels between thirteen. So the men quickly arranged themselves into groups of thirteen, collected their boxes and settled down to their share out operation. It was easy to share the cigarettes and sweets, and in Ian's group at least, these were shared first. The half-dozen sweets each man received were immediately in mouths, being chewed and enjoyed with relish because the virtual absence of sugar in the men's diet had caused them to crave sweet foods. Most of them had consumed all their sweets before the tins of food could be shared fairly, because there was some debate about how to do that.

But an amicable share out of the tins of food, involving some coin tossing, was achieved easily enough in the end. Then someone read the instructions on the wrapping which had been on each sweet. They were vitamin sweets to be eaten no more frequently than one every other day – and most of them had consumed all their five or six in a mere twenty minutes. What a waste. And that was not all, because most of them had a severe bout of squitters the next day.

The men had been prisoners for two and a half years and this was the second time they had received Red Cross supplies, the first occasion being in Singapore almost two years earlier when they each had about thirty cigarettes and only one or two tins of food. The bounty on this second occasion amounted to about twenty cigarettes, half a dozen vitamin sweets and two or three tins of food per man. They knew, and had known all the time, that the Imperial Japanese Army was officered and led by thieves who caused men to die from malnutrition and others from disease – since they also stole Red Cross medicines – because of their moral delinquency. So much for the IJA's much proclaimed Spirit of Bushido.

In October the Japanese ordered the digging of a trench around the entire camp perimeter. It was to be three metres wide and deep and the excavated earth was to be piled on the outside edge. The digging had to take place for three hours each evening after the men returned from their normal everyday work. Supervision by the guards ensured that men laboured hard all the time and before long the trench had progressed sufficiently for the IJA to deem it worthwhile to set up machine-gun posts at the four corners. When the trench was deeper than head height progress slowed because of the increased difficulty of throwing each spadeful of earth onto the pile already towering on the outside edge. The difficulty was compounded by the heavy clay subsoil whose stickiness enabled it to cling to the spade, in seeming stubborn refusal to be thrown. Whilst digging one evening, about twenty RAF four-engine bombers flew low over the course of the river – which was about three hundred yards away – and towards Kanchanaburi. The men were confident the RAF was aware of the identity of the camp and that they would not be targeted. Whilst they knew it would be unacceptable to the guards to be overtly joyful, their happiness at the sight of those bombers was considerable, and none missed the implications of the inability of the enemy to oppose them, either in the air or by anti-aircraft fire from the ground.

The purpose of the trench was all too obvious. It was not simply another means of fencing the men in; it was there to contain the men so that there could not be a breakout if and when the IJA ordered the massacre of the POWs in the camp. And after that,

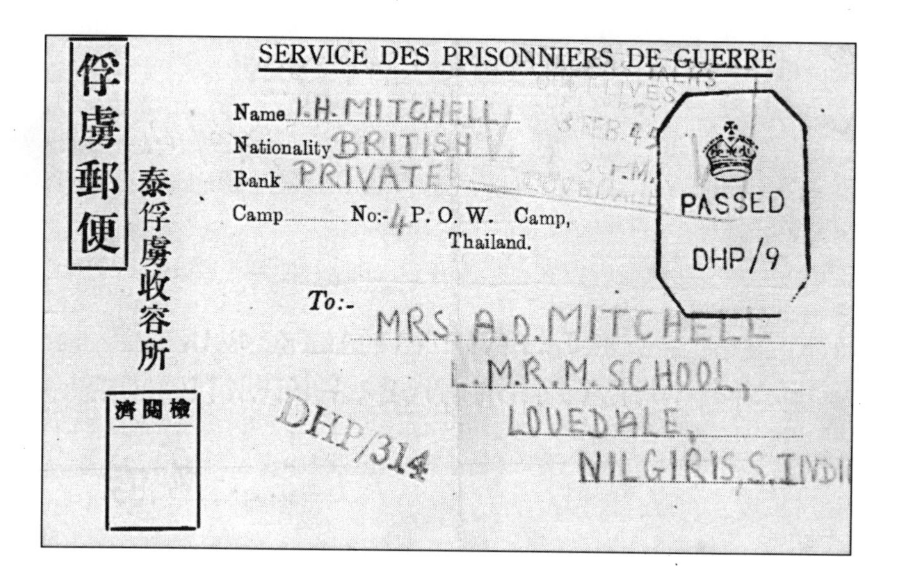

俘虜郵便

泰俘虜收容所

SERVICE DES PRISONNIERS DE GUERRE

Name I.H. MITCHELL

Nationality BRITISH

Rank PRIVATE

Camp .... No:- 4 P. O. W. Camp, Thailand.

PASSED DHP/9

DHP/314

To:- MRS. A.D. MITCHELL
L.M.R.M. SCHOOL,
LOVEDALE,
NILGIRIS, S. INDI

IMPERIAL JAPANESE ARMY

Date 10/6/44

Your mails (and PHOTOS) are received with thanks.
My health is (good, ~~usual, poor~~).
~~I am ill in hospital.~~
~~I am working for pay (I am paid monthly~~ salary).
I am not working.
My best regards to JEAN, AUNT ALEX, JUNE, ELSIE, WINSTON, SPENCER + KIRKMOUNT.

Yours ever,

Ian H. Mitchell

Note Ian's attempt to show that he was in good spirits by including Winston Spencer Churchill's name – in code.

it could be their grave. On occasions, some guards enjoyed themselves telling the men what they already knew.

In Tamuang camp was a man, Private Charles Letts, a Briton who had been a businessman in Bangkok. He had fled Thailand when the Japanese invaded that country at the outbreak of the Japanese war, and in Malaya had joined the SSVF. He was a fluent Thai speaker who regularly went out at night to bring in money and medical supplies, but mostly money, with which supplies were purchased for the camp hospital. His nocturnal excursions had been going on for quite some time. The trench would make his trips to and from camp much more difficult and dangerous. Ian, and many others in camp, had been aware what the brave man was doing. Most did not know if his excursions continued, or if they were prevented by the wide and deep trench. The trench did not, in fact, deter him and his excursions continued. It was said that he pole-vaulted across the ditch.

News from Tamarkan camp of an air raid in their vicinity was received in Tamuang. The Japanese had placed oil storage drums and their other army stores in an area adjacent to the camp; twenty four-engine bombers had flown low over the camp and attacked the supplies. Some bombs hit the camp causing POW casualties. Later it was established there had been eighteen POW deaths and seventy wounded.

Although there was confidence in Tamuang that the identity of their camp must already be known to the RAF and that they would not become a target, permission was sought to dig shallow trenches near to each hut. The IJA turned down the request – which was no surprise to anyone. Their logic had probably been very simple: the camp terrain was flat, and the only shields from machine-gun fire were flimsy bamboo huts, so why should the Japanese permit trenches in which men could shelter in the event of a future IJA decision to kill them all?

A party of POWs returned to camp after completing a repair job on the railway many miles upriver. They had a tale of terror to tell. As was usual they were travelling back to Tamuang by train, perched on the roofs of goods wagons. Three four-engine bombers flew over and circled, so the Japanese engine driver stopped the train and fled into the jungle, followed by the men's guards. The joyful POWs stayed on the wagon roof, cheering and waving until the planes, low and in line, approached the train and sticks of bombs were seen to be released; the train was on an embankment but even so the men jumped off and the bombs exploded as the men hit the ground. All the bombs missed the train and fell on one side of the embankment. The men fled into the jungle, taking with them such casualties as they could, and went back for more between breaks in the machine-gun fire from the planes – the bombers had flown over again to bomb the train successfully. The planes then circled for thirty minutes machine-gunning the jungle in which the men remained hidden.

After the planes had finally departed the men, and their guards, returned to the vicinity of the train. They tended the wounded as best they could, but since they had no medical supplies at all, their help was very restricted. The dead were buried beside the track. The men remained beside the destroyed train for a day, until another train arrived from the south, so that the journey south to Tamuang could be continued. The camp mourned the deaths and everyone had great sympathy for the survivors, whether wounded or physically unhurt.

The men told of the determined effort to destroy the train, particularly the engine, and all soon realised the strategy had probably changed. The Allies had become aware that their strategic bombing of the railway had limited impact because damage was repaired quickly. Therefore they would target rolling stock instead of bridges, because there was no chance that the Japanese could replace such stock, especially engines; subsequent bombings of rolling stock confirmed that assumption.

The increased frequency of bombing raids in the vicinity of Kanchanaburi and elsewhere was a tonic to the men. During the first two years or so of their imprisonment they had never seen or heard Allied aircraft – now there were huge, low-flying Allied aircraft which were totally unopposed, and absolutely no sight ever of Japanese aircraft, or even of anti-aircraft fire. Not even an extreme pessimist could miss the indication that the Japanese were very much on the run. The only real worry the men had now was that they would be massacred were the Allies to invade Thailand.

It was mid-December 1944 and the Japanese called for another working party of three hundred for a construction job upcountry. Ian and his brother Ron were included in the party; Ian was apprehensive because he knew of his physical limitations, but recognised that not being in a camp surrounded by a deep and wide trench, at a critical time, might be no bad thing. Ron was keen to go; he relished the prospect of a change of scenery and felt that change helped to speed the passage of time for him.

CHAPTER 6

Wampo-Tavoy Road

THE WORKING PARTY LEFT TAMUANG CAMP for the station about a mile away, as darkness fell, just a few days before Christmas.

The Japanese no longer used the railway in daylight because the RAF's strategy to destroy rolling stock was patently clear. The IJA hoped the cover of darkness would protect their precious stock. The men reached the station and awaited the train from Ban Pong; when it arrived the guards started their usual shouting and hustling while the men clambered onto the roofs of the wagons. The shouting and hustling were entirely unnecessary – all knew what was required of them – but it was an unpleasant habit the guards had taught themselves and grown into, so that it had become automatic behaviour for all occasions. About thirty men were on the roof of each wagon, and the wagons were full of oil drums.

The train moved off slowly and jerkily, pulled by an old engine fuelled with what seemed to be freshly felled green wood; the engine belched large sparks. As momentum was gained, speeds up to fifteen miles an hour were reached. By then the giant sparks which were spat upwards by the engine rained down on the unfortunate men on those wagon roofs. On each wagon the men huddled, holding on grimly to one another to ensure they stayed aboard the swaying, lurching wagon. They were wrapped in their blankets, made from hessian rice sacks, because December nights in that part of Thailand were cold. As the sparks showered down on them they had to choose between retaining their grip of the fellow they held onto for safety, or brushing off the burning and still live sparks. If the train was in the middle of a severe swaying or lurching spell, the burning spark had to be suffered stoically until smoother times; but there were occasions when near panic set in because one or more blankets were aflame and something had to be done about it quickly, lurch or no lurch. And all the time, amid the hazards of sparks, the danger of being thrown off the roof and the need to shelter from the biting cold, the men gazed skywards hoping not to see big four-engine bombers, because the sky was clear, the moon bright and the showers of sparks from the train could probably be seen from a mile high.

They had organised a system for plane spotting in which each man had responsibility as a look-out for a specified direction, which meant that an unfortunate few had to face to the rear, and it was more difficult to deal with sparks burning one's back. Ironically, men who wanted to smoke could not do so, not because they did not have a light, which had been a perpetual problem in POW camps because matches and lighters were not permitted, but because they did not have enough hands.

As the train lurched and swayed and went round bends for which the camber seemed adverse, men knew they were reaping what they had partly sown. The uneven track and the adverse cambers were to some extent, perhaps significantly so, due to the handiwork of men who sabotaged the embankments as they built them. They had incorporated and buried into the embankments such unstable materials as tree branches still wearing their leaves, the trunks of wild banana trees which were ninety-five per cent water, tangled vines, hollow bamboo and any other rubbish they could find. They had done this both as an act of sabotage and also to help them to achieve their daily quota of work – and some had said they did it specially for the emperor because it helped to speed up the construction of the railway! Generally, the men were pleased with their war efforts because the track really was in a bad way, which minimised train speed considerably. Here and there they passed wagons, and the occasional engine, which had fallen off the track and been left to rot because there was no lifting gear to replace them on the line.

The train reached the viaduct round the face of the cliff by the river's edge at Wampo South, the rickety looking construction which Ian, and everyone else, hoped they would never have to traverse, particularly on a train. The train slowed, almost to a stop, and then crept over the viaduct very, very slowly. The men remained silent. It was not the time to chat, joke, laugh or sing, nor was it a good thing to look over the edge at the rocks and river some frightening distance below. It seemed an appropriate time only to shut one's eyes in urgent prayer.

Eventually the viaduct was traversed. Silent were the sighs of relief, because macho men did not wish to give the game away. But the clown who unnecessarily reminded them that there would, hopefully, be a return journey in due course, did not draw a laugh or any comment. The need to re-cross the viaduct, at some future time, had been foremost in minds at the same time as those silent sighs of relief and thanksgiving for a safe crossing were being made.

Just a few miles more and the train stopped; they were at Wampo, and the men were required to dismount. They walked down the jungle path which had once been familiar to some of them, to the site of the former camp where some of the men had lived for some months, two years earlier. The jungle had reclaimed the territory which it had temporarily lost for the creation of the camp. Where there had been huts and a parade ground, substantial growth including trees well past sapling stage covered the former camp site. Dawn had broken and they were taken to the river beach, and there consumed the cooked rice they had brought with them. The only feature still unchanged was that small sandy beach where the men had walked ashore from the barge into the campsite more than two years earlier. That beach was a natural one and nature still preserved it in the same state. Ian had memories of the beach. He recalled the occasion when he had foolishly plunged into the river there in pursuit of fish after the Japanese had blasted the river with dynamite, and nearly drowned. He recalled also his days in the camp hospital, which had been just beyond the landward edge of the beach, when he had spent many peaceful hours with a string and bent pin and a supreme optimism that he might catch a fish some day.

The men were taken by barge to the other side of the river, the west bank, and disembarked immediately opposite the former Wampo camp. They were told they were required to build a road from there, through into Burma, to meet up with a road to the port of Tavoy, in the south-eastern part of Burma.

No great intelligence was required to discern that the RAF's attention to the railway had denied the Japanese much of the use of that supply route to their army in Burma. The road from Wampo to Tavoy was to be a branch supply route, or possibly the route their soldiers would take if driven out of Burma. The Japanese would be able to bring supplies by rail from Thailand to the Wampo end of the planned road, or by barge if the line from Kanchanaburi to Wampo could not be used. They instinctively knew that the construction of the road was likely to be another speedo job.

The Medical Officer who had travelled with them from Tamuang was Captain Pitt, and he was destined to remain behind at the camp beside the river, which was dubbed Wampo West. A medical orderly, a corporal in the RAMC, would accompany the first party of thirty into the jungle, and remain with them in a small jungle camp.

The party of thirty formed, and included Ron and Ian. They

were lined up opposite piles of tools, sacks of rice, tents, some live pigs encased in close fitting tubular carrying cases made from cane, live chickens in baskets, and sacks of brown sugar and dried fish. The whole of all that had been divided into lots of approximately equal weight, and with them were fifteen stout bamboo poles about seven or eight feet in length. The approximate weight of a load was well in excess of one hundred and fifty pounds. The officer spoke English and he ordered the men to form pairs, each pair to carry a load suspended from a bamboo pole, which the pair would shoulder.

The men viewed with disbelief and dismay the loads they were expected to carry and some started muttering; the officer angrily ordered the guards to fix bayonets. Captain Pitt intervened by asking the officer how far into the jungle the men had to carry the loads, and the answer shook them all. 'Twenty-two kilometres, exactly,' said the officer. The men left the talking to the Captain, who argued with the Japanese officer. But he was adamant – and the men all knew he would not change his mind because he could not be seen to give way to POWs in front of his soldiers – but Captain Pitt was also determined to have the last word. The Japanese officer told the Captain to stop arguing or he would lose his head, and he fingered the handle of his sword hanging from his waist to make the point. The Captain said, 'If you chop off my head, I'll tell Mr Churchill.' The Japanese pointed out that if his head was chopped off he would not be able to use mouth or tongue to tell anyone anything. Captain Pitt, still determined to have the last word, said, 'My men will tell Mr Churchill.' The officer strode off, but not before he instructed the guards, who advanced towards the men who were muttering.

Then a seemingly inexplicable event happened. A Sikh, an officer in British army uniform, clean and immaculate, strode into the jungle clearing from apparently nowhere. He walked confidently between the line of men and the advancing guards. Then as he faced the men, and without altering his stride, he said in good English, 'Keep your chins up, Britishers. Keep your chins up.' He continued walking and disappeared into the jungle on the path which the men were to take.

In a twinkling they sensed that a small British army unit was nearby on a mission behind enemy lines. The Sikh officer knew that if he was seen by the Japanese he would be mistaken for a soldier of the Japanese sponsored Indian National Army. He had watched the POWs and the trouble they were in, and had stepped out to steady them before blood was spilt. No one thought that there could be any other explanation.

The pairs of men pushed their bamboo poles through their tied-up loads and set off along the jungle path. They were mostly silent, but the occasional loud curse indicated that a toe had been stubbed in the rough terrain, or that worse had happened. From the guards, particularly from one of them who was soon dubbed 'The Natterer', came an endless exhortation to go faster. The men neither marched nor walked, they trotted – but with a wobbly, almost staggering, gait – for most of the time. But in places the course of the path was up steep banks, and the poor fellows at the back end of the poles had undue weight to bear. The bamboo poles were springy and the men soon developed bruises and blisters on their shoulders; they frequently moved the pole from one shoulder to the other for relief. And all the time the guards, who carried nothing but their rifles, nagged and nattered as they pressured for greater speed. The loads were heavy and awkward, the rough and uneven path through the jungle made the task a tough one, curses and expletives became more frequent.

Every hour or so the guards allowed a ten minute break. On stretches where progress was slowed by difficult terrain, the hour was stretched to seventy or more minutes. Ian and Ron shared a load and they seemed to fare no worse than many pairs, but the trek tested all the men severely. All in the party were strangers to most of the others, and had met for the first time when assembled to march out of Tamuang camp. But bonds were quickly formed by men who encouraged one another during the trek, and who were helpful during the rest breaks.

The guards had not previously had charge of POWs, so dialogue was difficult. But they must have been briefed about two words, 'Okay' and 'Speedo', which would more than get them by for the time being.

The trek had commenced at about eight in the morning and, but for the brief rest breaks, had continued hour after exhausting hour. At dusk the men had still not reached their destination and the guards kept on driving them. Then they were halted, for an overdue rest they thought, but soon realised that they had arrived at the destination, a spot in the jungle beside a gentle stream.

There was much to do before they could rest for the night. Two tents had to be erected, rice had to be cooked, a latrine had to be dug. The men, though very weary, tackled those chores urgently and with relief, because they looked forward to a good night's rest which would follow. And they were also relieved that the Japanese had indicated they could rest for two days whilst they organised their camp. The next day was Christmas Eve, and they could enjoy it, and Christmas Day, too. Since this place in the jungle had no name, the men named their camp Christmas camp.

By the evening of Christmas Day the men had got to know one another well, and firm friendships began to develop. Well after dusk another party of thirty, escorted by three guards, trekked past the camp. They were Dutch prisoners, and the men in Christmas Camp lined the path to greet them and to offer them a drink of boiled water if they were allowed to stop. But they were kept on the move. The Dutch carried comparatively light loads, perhaps because they had further to go. They were weary, but none as weary as one of their guards whose rifle was carried for him by a POW; the men from Christmas camp laughed heartily, and mockingly encouraged the guard to keep on. The pity of it all was that the guard had no previous experience of POWs and probably did not know that he was being ridiculed.

On the afternoon of Christmas Day the men had prepared twin campfires, one on either side of a clearing they planned to use as their stage for an impromptu concert that evening. After the Dutch party had trekked past they started with a sing-song. The four Japanese in the camp emerged from their tent to view the proceedings and, as was usual for Japanese who had not had previous contact with British POWs, were puzzled; how could soldiers who had surrendered rather than commit *hara kiri* sing and be joyful when they were so disgraced? That had been the common question asked by guards new to POWs, and it was asked again, but politely this time. The men understood the question, they knew some Japanese words and almost expected it to be asked. But in order not to offend, they only smiled when told that Japanese soldiers never surrender because they preferred death.

The guards did not spoil the party – they seemed to enjoy it, too, which had also usually happened in previous camps with other guards – and it went on cheerfully and noisily. There were no musical instruments in the camp, but that did not reduce the capacity of the men to sing with some melody, and very loudly. Patriotic songs were sung, of course, but so were 'She'll be coming round the mountain', 'Nellie Dean', 'Knees up Mother Brown' – which was danced with vigour by Archie Gibson and Les Wandless – and other lively numbers. The Japanese sergeant particularly liked 'Knees up Mother Brown' and 'She'll be coming round the mountain' and his request to sing them again was happily met; the knees-up jig by Archie and Les made his day. Monologues were recited, and even in that small gathering there was someone who knew the verses of 'Eskimo Nell and Dead Eye Dick', 'The Green Eye of the Little Yellow God' and other classics of the British army. It was recalled that in Wampo camp, two years earlier, Colonel Lilly had banned the reciting of 'Eskimo Nell' because of its obscenity, but it had since been heard so often that its obscenity was overlooked in the admiration for its crudity, simplicity and manifest humour. And, with the exception of drunken army messes, could there be a more suited occasion for its recitation, than before thirty British POWs deep in the Thai jungle, who had been captive for thirty-four months, and had already been to hell!

It was past midnight when the party was over. The men, tired but at least at ease with themselves, slept peacefully. The Japanese had stipulated that apart from one man whom the men could appoint as their cook, all, including the medical orderly, had to work on the road from the day after Christmas. So the men were awakened early in the morning. The cook had already boiled their rice, so after a quick wash by the little stream, they breakfasted and were ready for roll-call and work.

They learnt, with some relief, that the 'road' to be built was to be only a track, three metres wide on flat terrain and two metres wide in the hills. Their task in that camp was to complete a stretch of eight miles, four to the east and four to the west of the camp. The terrain they were on was generally flat, but there were gullies they had trekked over, and perhaps the terrain to the west of them would not be much different, but the jungle was dense enough to prevent a view of any significant distance.

The senior POW was a Company Sergeant Major. The guard in charge of the work was a sergeant from the Japanese engineering regiment, who quickly impressed the men with his expertise at primitive engineering and innovative skills. No one could pronounce his name, and since he seemed a decent enough fellow, they named him Tom. Another guard who always looked in pain and spent much time unsuccessfully trying to pee, was dubbed Gonners. The Natterer had been named during the trek, leaving only one more name to be bestowed, but this was not an urgent matter and it seemed proper to delay the christening until the nature of the guard was known.

The work was heavy, but not unpleasant because the weather was dry and Tom was not unreasonable. Good progress was made on the first morning – at least Tom seemed pleased enough with it – and the men were rewarded with a ten minute break after each hour's work. This was seemingly traditional in the Japanese army, unless a speedo was the order of the day. As long as Tom was around the Natterer was reasonably silent, but during any absence of the sergeant he seemed to take it upon himself to carry on endless grumbling and hassling sessions. The men generally tried to ignore his annoying habit, perhaps their attitude to him made him worse – but most of them did not think his bad habit was altered one jot by their attempts generally to ignore the fellow.

The men had each brought out with them a dollop of rice in their mess-tins – for their lunch – as was the usual practice in working camps. At about mid-day the lunch break was authorised by Tom and he inquisitively went over to have a look at the men's food. He seemed surprised and shook his head – in disbelief, it seemed – as he walked away. When he had finished eating he went over to the men and gave one of them a tasty morsel, which it was thought he had set aside expressly for a POW. On subsequent days he often repeated the gesture. At six in the evening the day's work ended and the men returned to camp, which was nearby, because they had commenced at the camp and progressed eastwards for only some hundreds of yards.

It was convenient for the men that the little stream was adjacent to the camp site. There were no restrictions on washing and generally refreshing themselves, other than the obvious requirement to do it downstream of the well which had been dug in the stream so that buckets of water could easily be scooped for kitchen use.

The men were not surprised that none of the cooking oil, brown sugar, dried fish, chickens or pork was destined for them. That was par for the course. So was the men's intent to supplement their diet when opportunity presented itself. But the general view was that nothing should be stolen from the Japanese cookhouse, because such a theft in a camp with only thirty-one POWs would be too incriminating. There was not even a nearby Thai village which might deflect the Japanese from their probable certainty that any loss should be laid at the door of the POWs.

There were some outstanding characters in Christmas camp. Archie Gibson was a cheerful Londoner with ready wit, an even readier smile, a kindly and generous disposition and an unfailingly optimistic outlook. Archie's friend, Bill Saxton – who in happier days was a bank manager in Brighton – was also a man of good cheer and wit, a kindly, considerate man who chuckled readily and had a bubbling, effervescent personality. His parents were probably clairvoyants, because his third forename was Bubbles, it genuinely was one of the names he was christened with. Taffy Minton was, of course, a Welshman, who had been a coal miner and a councillor in his home town. He was well informed about life and politics; wise, cheerful, interesting, he was always helpful and kind, and the stories he told of his life, and of South Wales, were splendid to listen to. He was also a happy person who was a joy to behold, with his two front teeth whose prime and prominent function seemed to be to light up an ever cheerful face. John Hinde was a business executive in Singapore, quiet, seemingly studious and a very unlikely soldier; he was mature, thoughtful, considerate, never spoke a harsh word or swore and certainly never uttered any expletive. There were two sergeants who were friends – like Laurel and Hardy, many thought, because one was fat and the other thin – and they were often cheerfully, but seriously, disagreeing. They were a delight to know because of their good cheer and general optimism.

There were others, too, and in total the men in that camp had cause to be grateful that so many of them were delightful comrades and they got on so well together. There was only one unfortunate exception, a miserable loner who seemed unable, or unwilling, to respond to gestures of comradeship, even seemed suspicious of them. But though the men were a little sorry for him, none let his presence affect them.

Work continued daily and the men's respect and liking for Tom grew. He was a decent fellow, immensely hardworking and physically strong with rippling muscles in body and limbs. The muscles of his neck and those on top of his shoulders were remarkably pronounced. He never nagged or scolded, but was the first and only Japanese the men had ever known always to knuckle down to the work himself; all regarded him as a good guy. There were days when he was absent, probably surveying and marking out the route the track was to take, or helping with the field telephone which was being installed to link all the camps on the route to Tavoy. On those days the working atmosphere was unpleasant because the Natterer nattered endlessly and endeavoured to make the men acknowledge his presence. Sometimes Tom was temporarily replaced by another sergeant, who was called Happy Days, because he was so miserable. Some said his name related to the fact that, as a non-smoker, he was not even able to offer bribes. But he really was an unhappy fellow. He was never as bad as the guards the men had known on the railway, but he was intimidating if the men slackened off or were slowed by an obstacle. His name suited him well, and the song 'Happy Days Are Here Again' was sung by a look-out as a warning, whenever he was seen returning after any absence during the working day.

But more often than not Tom was there and things went well. He relished building small, sturdy bridges over the deep gullies, and had considerable experience in design and building. He could also show off his remarkable strength when heavy tree trunks had to be dragged or carried to the site and manoeuvred into position. The only POW there who could match and surpass Tom's strength was Preston, a glutton for really heavy work. Ian had seen Preston in a dysentery ward at Chungkai about a year earlier, and he was then mere skin and bone – the transformation in his physique, and his immense strength, astounded him. Preston was certainly not troubled with any weakness in his limbs, as Ian was.

During their work one day they had hastily to step aside when confronted by a herd of some fifty cattle bearing down upon them, driven by a Japanese soldier. The cattle were in a state of near exhaustion, as was the soldier; and all looked as though a rest and a long drink would do them a power of good. Some of the animals had half sacks of rice strapped onto their backs. It was evident that the animals were being driven into Burma to feed the Japanese forces there. The episode was repeated the following week, excepting that none was loaded with sacks. There was, however, an additional factor – the leading animal had a bamboo cane strapped to its horns, projecting eighteen inches beyond the beast's nose, and from it a banana dangled. Someone remarked that the ploy would never work because the banana was not peeled. The animals, and the Japanese soldier, looked nearly exhausted. An idea was hatched during the rest of that day's work, and it was agreed to put it to Tom at the end of the day.

That evening sergeants 'Laurel' and 'Hardy', with Les Wandless who had a great deal of cockney wit and cheek, asked Tom if it would be OK for the men to rustle a beast the next time cattle were driven past. Tom chuckled with amusement. His face lit with fun, he thought for a whole half minute and then agreed. Les generously offered to give any portion of the animal the Japanese favoured, and Tom's amusement was hard for him to constrain. But he returned to the men later and warned them that if they were caught by a Japanese officer they would be shot. He stipulated therefore that the beast had to be taken at least half a mile away into the jungle to be killed and cooked there, and all the residue had to be buried there too. None of the cooked meat, not even the broth, could be stored in the camp. If they were caught he said he would deny all involvement, and they would be on their own. The men expressed gratitude for his warning and for his kindness, and assured him that no risks would be taken. But all knew the venture could not be undertaken without risks, and no one asked for the idea to be abandoned.

Now the men had to plan how the deed should be done. Ian knew the best way to do it. It was so simple he could not understand why everyone else had not also jumped to the same solution. The cattle were exhausted on both previous occasions, so it could be expected that they would be in that same condition the next time. The beasts would be very thirsty and one of them could easily be led off if tempted with a bucket of water. Furthermore, the act of tempting the animal away could easily be carried out in a seemingly innocent fashion. The plan was accepted even before he could boast of the absolute merits of the scheme. Since it was his idea, he insisted on the honour of being the hero who would do the deed, and his democratic comrades agreed without dissent.

Every day Ian carried out a bucket of water and a length of cord with him as they marched off to work, much to Tom's chuckled amusement. The men formed the opinion that Tom must have told the other guards about the plot, and that they were none too happy about it – which was not at all surprising because of the trouble which could lie ahead. Sure enough, one afternoon the approach of driven cattle could be heard. Ian rushed to the strategic place he had reckoned was most suited for the adventure he had looked forward to so much. He had planned to approach the tail end of the herd where there would be stragglers, probably more desperate for water than the others – he had thought. He would walk into the jungle just as soon as an animal took an interest in his bucket, and he would seemingly be unaware that he was being followed. When out of sight of the Japanese drover he would rope the beast, and his job would be done. But as soon as he was near enough for a straggler to smell the water, the entire herd also smelled it and there was a minor stampede towards him and his bucket. He dropped the bucket and climbed a tree, which was the wisest thing he could think of in a hurry! No one laughed more heartily than Tom. The POWs had less to laugh about – an opportunity to taste beef had been wasted.

It was realised that cattle were driven past the camp about every fifth day, so the men had time to devise another subtle way to gain a bull. They hit upon the simplest and surest way. Two men armed with sledgehammers would both cripple the same animal by smashing its front knees, and six men would be ready to drag the creature into the jungle. The selected animal would be one near the front of the herd, out of view of the drover at the back. Later, as many men as required would carry the animal to the place in the jungle of which Tom had already approved. Stout bamboo poles and ropes were available to aid them.

On the expected day the herd arrived and the plan was effected successfully. In due course the men had stewed beef for two days, even for breakfast, and broth for supper. The Japanese cookhouse chose the liver and a choice piece of meat and were pleased – because their supply of chickens and pigs had been exhausted some days earlier. The POWs could have made their beef last longer, but risks had to be minimised and they also knew that another herd would be along soon enough. The men made a show of working harder and more cheerfully to show Tom their appreciation, and everything was fine. The rustling continued whenever a herd was driven past. On occasions two beasts were mistakenly crippled, due to confusion rather than greed, so there was often a live bull already in the jungle hide-out, queuing for the stew pot.

1 January 1945 had come and gone and the men wondered if this was going to be the year that the war would end. They hoped their road would be completed and that they would have left that vicinity before the Japanese retreat from Burma started – they clearly did not think much of their chances if trapped near the path of retreating Japanese units. And they thought the retreat might be soon because the unopposed Allied air activity over Thailand was a powerful indication to the men that the enemy was taking a beating in Burma. In fact, was it not possible, even probable, that their road was intended more for a retreat than for a supply route? They knew they had cause for concern.

Such worrying thoughts always troubled the men. But they dared not flee into the jungle prematurely, because they would be hunted down and killed; and if they were not caught, it was unlikely that they could survive for long without food or the means of trapping food. Furthermore, there might well be reprisals against other POWs, to teach all a lesson. Indeed they were certain that reprisals against others would follow if, to facilitate their flight into the jungle, they killed or injured any Japanese. The men did discuss the possibilities and were generally aware of the need to be alert to any eventuality, because they knew their survival might depend on their alertness and willingness to make quick decisions.

News was received that a POW had been shot and killed in Tamuang on New Year's Eve. A drunken Japanese warrant officer had shot the man who was visiting the latrines. Other guards arrived to investigate the shot and he was seen by POWs to require them to drag the body to the perimeter fence, and to damage the fence so as to suggest that the man was escaping.

Work on the road continued apace and conditions had toughened; the working day had lengthened, rest periods were reduced in frequency and length, and the men were driven harder by additional guards. The field telephone system had been completed and care was needed to avoid breaking the suspended wire when felling trees. But the men had become very expert at tree felling and had a professional pride in making trees fall in their chosen direction. Tree felling was a task they preferred to any other, even though the axes were of poor quality and, nearly as bad, the Japanese saws had teeth designed to cut when pulling rather than pushing.

On one occasion, however, the men jockeyed to avoid having to fell a particular tree which overhung the telephone cable stretched out between smaller trees below. Each of them spun out the felling job they were on, delaying completion until someone had been assigned the overhanging tree, which would unavoidably break the telephone cable. Taffy Minton was the unfortunate who drew the short straw; he could not any longer delay the felling of the little tree he was chopping at, because the guard was onto him, urging him to speedo. He was given the awkward tree to fell.

Taffy tried to explain to the guard that there was no way in which the tree could be felled without breaking the telephone cable. But the guard was adamant that it could be done, and as Tom was not there that day there was no worthwhile Japanese to appeal to. That guard must have had immense faith in the men's skills to control the direction of the fall of trees. Or, perhaps he had not heard of the law of gravity. The tree had a serious lean, causing it to tower over the telephone line, and the bursting of the cable would be an inevitable consequence of the tree being felled. Taffy was ordered to start chopping.

What was about to happen was beyond doubt. The tree would break the cable, the guard would know that his seniors would blame him, so he would beat up Taffy in order to feel better. And by so doing, he would reckon to avoid some loss of face in front of the men, because it would show them that he still knew the tree could have been made to fall the other way. Japanese behaviour was often as predictable as that.

As he chopped away Taffy could see the funny side of what would be a hilarious scene, were it not for the certainty that he would suffer at the end of it. He, as much as any other man there, had sought to avoid that tree, knowing that if he avoided it successfully, someone else would be in the stew. He knew he had simply drawn the short straw and that when the day was over his leg would be pulled unmercifully, unless, of course, the beating was severe, in which case he would draw sympathy. He hoped, therefore, that at the end of the day, and probably for a few days after, the others would feel able to pull his leg.

The tree was felled and all around stopped work to watch it fall, not because of Taffy's warning shout of 'T-I-M-B-E-R!' All knew where that tree would fall, and it would not be in their direction. The guard seemed as though he wanted to tear his hair out; Taffy knew there was no point in attempting to tell the guard, 'I told you so.' No one had ever been foolish enough to learn the Japanese expression for that, so he did not know the words even if he was suicidal enough to want to say it, and he was not. So he put on the sad, helpless look and was only given a slapping. The men were not deprived of the fun they would have at his expense that evening, and for many days thereafter. Taffy was a real man, a very nice person whom everyone liked and had great respect for. He was also an entertaining story teller, and none had any doubt that that incident would be added to his repertoire of stories, and he would tell it well. But even so, no one suggested to him that he might, therefore, be glad it had happened.

For whatever reason, cattle had not been driven through for quite a few days and the men sensed that the beef bonanza was over for good. So they were back to the plain hopeless rice twice a day, and hopeless rice with a watery vegetable soup each evening. But they were soon to learn how fortunate they were that they no longer had beef in the stew pot. As they paraded for roll-call and work one morning, an excited guard ran from the Japanese tent and had an animated conversation with the guard taking the roll-call. Both guards looked worried, perhaps even frightened. They told the men that a telephoned message from Tom, who was then in the next camp up the road, warned that a Japanese officer on horseback was on his way to the camp to look for traces of cattle.

The men told the guards they understood the situation and that the guards could relax because nothing would be found. But their assurances failed to relieve the worried guards who had been required to keep the men in camp so that they would be available for the officer. The men knew they had to remain calm and confident, and if possible they had to transmit their calmness to the very frightened guards. They were expert at being POWs, which was just as well under the circumstances. They knew they should convey only a sense of mild inquisitiveness and puzzlement, if quizzed by the officer. They were also confident that the bruised jungle leading to the distant place where the animals had been butchered and the remains buried, was no longer bruised, and there would be nothing to lead the officer to that place.

The officer arrived and remained on his horse throughout. Obviously he would get a better view of the immediate surrounds to the camp from the high vantage point gained by being mounted on quite a big horse. He did not speak English – but all were aware that perhaps he might be fluent at it, and nothing careless should be said. He gave his instructions through the guards. He looked angry, fierce and very, very cruel. He was alert, his eyes took in every detail, his orders to the guards were cold and clinical and he carefully watched the outcomes. He also searched the men's faces, seeming to be looking for an indication of guilt. His first order to the men was to remove the smouldering ashes from the campfire, and he demanded that they dig three feet down under the site of the fire. After that he inspected the open kitchen area and the men had to dig again under the location of the kitchen fire. After this the men were made to spread the pig swill, and dig in the swill pit until he could see the bottom was untouched soil. The officer then made an inspection of the borders of the camp and surrounding jungle, also examining the stream. Still not satisfied, he returned to camp and instructed the men to make bamboo probes, each with a hooked end. He watched over them as he directed a systematic trawl through the contents of the latrine trench with the probes, a search which lasted some twenty minutes. Finally he rode off without even saying so much as, 'Sorry I troubled you.'

There was no joy when he left, only intense relief that they had got away with it. The guards, obviously relieved, were quite animated. The shaking of their heads, their chatter and the pursing of their lips suggested that they were saying the equivalent of 'Phew'. The men felt they owed Tom a lot for their deliverance, because it was he who had insisted that the animals be taken at least half a mile away for retention and slaughter, and that all the bones and skin had to be buried there too. But for that, the bones might well have ended under the campfire, and would then certainly have been found.

Tom came back to the camp that evening specially to tell the men there must be no more rustling, ever. He seemed to be saying 'Phew', in cheerful and friendly fashion. The men knew how narrow was their escape – if the driving of cattle past their camp had not ceased, the likely outcome would have been that evidence of beef in the kitchen would have been detected, and their troubles would have been serious, and terminal for some, at least.

One more incident with a bull occurred some three weeks later. The men were levelling a stretch of track – a pass – they had cleared of growth, at the foot of two hills which rose steeply on both sides to make a pass of about four hundred yards long. All thirty were at the eastern end, their guards with them, when a bull appeared at the western end of the pass, heading towards them. It was obviously a beast which had strayed from a herd being driven into Burma some weeks earlier. It was sturdy, fresh looking and had obviously fed well off the jungle vegetation. An instant decision was made to capture it, and all the men scurried up the hill out of sight of the bull. The party agreed that some would move west and come down behind the bull, and the rest on the eastern end of the pass would then come down to trap the animal between the two parties.

However things did not work strictly to plan. Only Ron and Ian went west and came down behind the bull, one with a sledgehammer, and one with an axe. The other twenty-eight had all remained at the eastern end and came down on to the track to close off that end of the pass; they were mostly armed with a variety of weapons including sledgehammers and axes. Hardly had the men started to close in when the bull turned about to face the two brothers, then it charged in their direction. The two men stood near the edges of the track, about five feet apart, and facing each other. They were both fixed on the need to stand their ground, remain calm and slay the bull as it charged between them, hopefully. The scene was something which might have had a proper place in a Western movie. The oncoming bull, charging with its head down, should have been a fearful sight to the brothers who would have been wise to flee up the hill. But they were young; there was the matter of doing their duty and not letting down their comrades. For those and any other reasons there might have been, they continued to hold their ground, and all the time the beast built up a ferocious momentum as it bore down towards them. Then, just as it should have done if playing a part in a Western, it skidded to a halt in a swirl of rising dust, nose close to the ground and forelegs outstretched, less than fifteen feet from the brothers. The twenty-eight at the other end were relieved for the sakes of Ron and Ian, but the sum total of their combined relief was certainly less than the relief felt by each of the brothers.

Then the animal turned about and again faced the twenty-eight. The outraged, or terrified, creature charged towards them with all the ferocity and momentum of its earlier charge – the men wisely fled up the hill – and continued its charge at least until it was well out of sight. The two guards, who had discreetly remained up the hill all of the time, could scarcely contain their merriment, but patted the brothers on the back. None of the twenty-eight said any words of praise to Ron and Ian, but neither did they remark on their absurd stupidity. And Ron and Ian knew that the others were right to flee because had they held their ground the twenty-eight men swinging axes, sledgehammers, picks and spades would have been a considerable hazard to one another.

But there was more to come. When they returned to camp that evening they were greeted by a very jubilant camp cook. 'You'll never believe it,' he said excitedly. 'I heard a thundering of hooves when I was at the stream, looked up, and there was this bloody bull tearing down the road towards me. It was still fifty yards away and I was working out which tree I should hide behind, when it dropped dead. The Jap cook and I carved it up, he took about a third and we've got the rest. It's true. I'm not kidding,' he said to the men who were less surprised than the cook had expected them to be.

Archie Gibson said what he had often said previously about very remarkable incidents, 'When I tell them about this at home after the war, it'll be worth a pint, at least, every time I tell it. And it's worth telling often.' But on these remarkable occasions there was always someone to remind him that after the war he would not be believed, even if some of his mates were kind enough to listen patiently to the veteran with the vivid imagination. Indeed that sentiment was probably voiced by most men in the camps in Thailand after each of many seemingly improbable incidents.

The guard who had slapped Taffy Minton for breaking the telephone cable when he felled a tree, was at it again. Two men had been assigned to fell a huge fig tree whose branches were draped in vines, some of which hung down to ground level; others were entwined in the branches of adjacent trees. They indicated that, in the interests of safety, they needed to chop off many of the vines before bringing down the tree. But the guard knew best and would have none of it; he stood nearby and made the men speedo after asking them the direction in which the tree would fall. He had then chosen a vantage point from which he could scream 'speedo'. A tree whose attached vines are enmeshed in branches of adjoining sturdy trees might be tugged by the vines as it starts its fall, and bounce back to fall in another unpredictable direction. But that would be too much to explain to an impatient guard who only understood basic words like 'OK' and 'speedo'. Nor could it readily be explained to such a person that the vines hanging down near him could whiplash to lift him off his feet as the tree fell.

In due course the huge tree began to move and the urgent cry of 'T-I-M-B-E-R!' rang out. The men in the vicinity fled on routes each of them had predetermined; only the small, helpless guard stayed where he was. Too late it dawned on him that he could be in trouble. He started to run, became mixed up with some of the hanging vines, and was hurled about twenty feet. Fortunately for him he sustained bruises rather than serious injuries. The men maintained their straight faces even though all of them had known at the time that he was overseeing the felling of that tree from a very unsafe place. The tree had fallen in the predicted direction, so the guard had no cause to slap anyone.

Some pigs had been brought from Wampo for the Japanese, but one of them escaped from its enclosure. The pig remained in the vicinity of the camp and was often seen feeding at the shallow swill pit used by the Japanese. They had tried to recapture it often enough, but it was a wily animal and had evaded them. No attempt was made to shoot it, which led the men into suspecting that ammunition was in very short supply and they were under orders not to use any. Tom was back in camp and he told the men they could have the pig if they could catch it. So after the day's work they filtered into the jungle and spread out to encircle the area surrounding the camp, hoping to drive the pig into the camp precincts where it could be trapped. They had no success at all, did not even see or hear the animal. But it had been fun and sergeant 'Hardy' had become entangled in a vine with itchy hairs – which instantly caused a severe itchy rash. Tom recommended that he should strip completely and rub ash all over himself, which he did with the help of 'Laurel', because no one knew that Tom was joking. And Tom, who had not realised his advice had been taken seriously, had returned to the Japanese quarters.

The sight of 'Hardy', nude and blackened with wood ash, was something worth beholding. The tubby fellow did not mind the laughter because he had faith in Tom's remedy and was confident that the itch would soon go. Hearing the peals of laughter the

Japanese emerged from their tents, and joined in. Tom must then have told his fellow guards of the joking advice he had given, because their laughter grew and seemed almost uncontrollable. Tom tried to explain to 'Hardy', but could not easily do so because he could not tame his merriment. The message was eventually delivered and 'Hardy' then spent quite some time washing off the ash; without soap it was not very easy. The rash and itch did not last through the night, but the fun was still there the next morning.

The workday was lengthened, rest breaks were shortened, and their frequency reduced. Obviously the guards had received orders to speed up the job. The inadequacy of their progress on the road construction was due partly, at least, to the fact that the site at which they worked became more distant from the camp each day. It had reached the point where it had become nearly a four mile walk from camp, which took time and energy to reach and return from. And possibly the strategic need for the road had become more urgent. The men were worked hard, and there were times when they feared that the project was sliding into the sort of scenario which had preceded the 'Speedo' on the railway job. Most thought the Japanese must have upgraded the urgency for strategic reasons. Whatever the reason, pressures to work harder, faster and longer seemed to grow by the day.

Even so, upon their return to camp each evening the men relaxed easily, probably because their guards were nothing like the vicious and cruel ones who had terrorised them in railway camps. The men usually brought back wood for the campfire, which was lit as soon as they returned. After eating their evening meal they would settle down in the dusk, or dark, in small groups playing cards or just talking. Unless there was something special to talk about concerning the war or their situation, they talked of their homes, families, jobs, hobbies, romances – and some became firm friends. It was during such chats in the early days in Christmas camp that it was learned that Bill Saxton's third forename was Bubbles, and that Archie Gibson would not disclose his second and third forenames – which must have been a leg-pull because they turned out to be very nice and ordinary names. Inevitably they also talked of food and of the foods they missed most. Some craved steaks, or juicy pork, or other rich foods; many, including Ian, dreamed only of fresh bread and butter.

One of the men had been a crew member of the *Empress of Asia*, the disgraced supply ship. Enough of its crew had mutinied to prevent it from entering Singapore's harbour because they had wanted to get out of that region fast. The ship had then been bombed and sunk and its supplies denied to the besieged defenders of Singapore. Generally men who knew of that mutiny – and most did – had a grudge against the seamen who sailed that ship. But this fellow was a cheerful chap, entertaining, full of humour, helpful, hardworking, optimistic and just as brave as all the others in the camp. He told them of the sinking, and of his rescue, and none of the men there had anything but normal respect and liking for the man, and knew they could rely on him as a buddy.

Ian had nominal charge of the camp fire and was pleased to be useful. It was also no bad thing that his sleeping place in the tent – which had no wall because it had been removed for convenience – was closest to the fire and near enough for him to benefit from the warmth of its flames or embers throughout the night. One cold night when the fire blazed merrily a guard awakened him, and all the others too, because an aircraft was high over camp. He was made to put out the fire, speedo. The men were not unduly bothered if the camp had been spotted because they were quite sure that the Allies must by then have been informed that POW camps were spread along the track between Wampo and Tavoy. Such was the confidence which had grown in the men. But they wondered what a lone aircraft was doing in the middle of the night speeding on its way high above the Thai jungle.

Two men in camp had reported sick. Bill Saxton's disability was worrying – his knees had swollen, they ached and he was unable to walk. It was evident, even to the Japanese, that he was unable to work. The second casualty was the friendless loner, who complained that his knees were weak and painful. The medical orderly could do nothing for either man. The loner was deemed fit for light work only. He usually hobbled around, but some had noticed him walk normally in the dark. He was not given the benefit of any doubt because of his character, and it was generally supposed that he was swinging the lead and had chosen symptoms which could not be disproved and which were vaguely similar to Bill's.

Bill's illness could not have come at a worse time. The stretch of track, which had been the men's task since their first days in Christmas camp, was just about completed. They had been told of a planned move for them, further west. They would leap-frog other camps and join a camp of Dutch POWs to help complete their section. They had only one more day in Christmas camp, then would have to pack and march.

The evening before their exit from Christmas camp a bamboo stretcher was made for Bill, so that he could be carried. He had become unable even to stand, but he still remained his usual happy, bubbly self; he never complained and was cheerfully grateful for help given him. The question was, who were the four lucky men to have the pleasure of carrying him on the march the next day? Everyone claimed to be a special friend of his and wanted to carry him. So Bill chose the four he wanted, and wisely selected sturdy fellows of about equal height, and included three who were only ordinary comrades. The men chosen were delighted, because Bill's weight was probably under ten stones, which meant that the weight each of the four would shoulder would be no more than thirty-five pounds, which was less than half the weight each of the rest would have to carry.

The march started early in the morning, the loads again being carried by pairs of men. Despite the number of men available for carrying being reduced by six – the two sick men and the four who carried Bill – the weight of loads shared between the remaining twenty-five was not much different to that carried on their trek from Wampo West to Christmas camp. That was because there was a great deal less food to carry. The men also knew that most of the route which lay ahead of them was prepared track. Without steep or slippery banks to climb, without surfaced tree roots and rocks to stumble over, or jungle vegetation to impede them, the trek would be considerably easier than the previous one. And, of course, the four carrying Bill would have it really easy – so they thought.

Within just a few hundred yards the stretcher bearers realised that their burden was a much heavier one than just the weight of Bill. The bamboo stretcher was springy and its bed was flat, lacking the inward slope of proper stretchers with canvas beds; much care was required to keep Bill aboard. One other problem was that the bearers could not individually change shoulders, but had to bear the discomfort and pain of the bouncy bamboo poles on a shoulder until the other bearers agreed it was time to lower the stretcher and swap positions. Positions were changed often, and the frequency of changes increased progressively because the discomfort and pain the bearers suffered was considerable. And each change sapped strength and stamina, not just because of the additional effort required to lower and lift the load, but mainly because their rhythm was interrupted. And all the time Bill implored the men to be more careful, pleading at times, as he gripped the stretcher to avoid falling off.

But there was worse to come, much worse. The men were soon in hilly country where the track zig-zagged its way up and down steep hills, with acute U-turns every four or five hundred yards so that users would not be confronted with excessively steep gradients. In hilly terrain like that, the track was only two metres wide and it was cut into the side of the hill; thus those tracks were bordered by a sheer wall of soil and rock on one side, and nearly a sheer drop on the other.

As soon as they were in the hills the bearers were in trouble, and Bill in near panic. The bearers on the outside edge of the track, aware of the sheer drop they were skirting, pushed inwards to gain a wider margin of safety. But the bearers on the inside, each of whose leg, hip and arm was bruised and torn more and more by rubbing against the rocky sub strata of the sheer wall they were being pushed into, pushed outwards for self preservation. The inside men were in permanent conflict with their mates on the outside, whose paramount concern, of course, was to avoid falling off the edge of the track and tumbling down the hill.

Bill Saxton, in a state of near terror, pleaded, begged, implored – but to no avail. He asked to be put down, promising to crawl all the way, but there was no chance of that happening. The bearers repeatedly changed sides, and just as often, wished they had not done so. One asked if there were any volunteers from the rest of the party who would take a turn on the stretcher, but none ever seemed to hear him although he made the plea frequently and loudly enough. The guards hardly helped – they constantly demanded speedo and were unhappy that the stretcher bearers slowed the progress of the trek. The Natterer was in his element.

During rest breaks the other men sought to encourage Bill and his bearers. 'It will be easier on the downhill, and that can't be far off because we're nearly at the top,' one man had said. But when challenged he could not explain why. They reached the top and rested, but there were at least five of them who could not care less about the splendid view.

The downhill sections were, of course, easier for all of them. But the stretcher party was still faced with the same problem. Bill's worries could not end until they were out of the hills, but they did not know that from there on there were only hills. At the top of one they saw a marker, and they knew that the boundary was crossed and that they were in Burma. The men were all greatly relieved when their destination was reached. It had been a very hard day's work for all of them, and an ordeal for some.

Their stay at the Dutch camp was brief. Just a few days there to complete that section and both parties, British and Dutch, were trekking again to share a camp well on the way to Tavoy. The Dutch camp they left had been beside a river and was thus easily supplied. The Japanese rations again included live pigs, chickens, dried fish, brown sugar and cooking oil, in addition to the sacks of rice. But evidently the expected stay at the next camp was to be a brief one because there was much less rice to carry than previously. Another pointer was that they carried only one tent – the one for the guards. Bill had recovered enough to walk unaided, which was a great relief – especially to him – but he was spared from carrying a load.

This time the men would not carry the pigs, chickens, sugar and fish simply for their guards to eat – they planned to get some of those goodies for themselves. There were four live pigs, each in a close fitting cylindrical cane basket carried on a bamboo pole on the shoulders of two men. The Brits had decided to kill a pig in the belief that the guards would then hand it over to them lest it had died of a sickness. But it would not be killed until late in the afternoon, so the meat would be fresh when they received it. Similarly the men carrying the basket of chickens would kill a couple late in the day.

The men who carried the dried fish and brown sugar would part the hessian sacking carefully – it was loosely woven – and extract reasonable amounts before rearranging the woven hessian so that pilfering would not be suspected. Those entrusted to that stealing did it early and shared out the stolen food amongst the others to conceal. The pig was duly killed by driving a bamboo spike into its brain via an ear, so the damage to the pig was not apparent. The chickens were suffocated, so they, too appeared undamaged.

The trek had been of the usual severity and the destination was not reached until well after nightfall. The camp site was a steep slope which overlooked a river just twenty yards away. The guards gave the dead pig and chickens to the men, and then erected their tent. The men slept in the open that night – the next day they could build themselves a shelter, using trees and bamboo from the jungle. It was a clear night, so there were no problems. The British and Dutch parties remained separate – even though sited adjacently – because that was the normal relationship for them. They cooked separately, roll-called separately, were administered separately and worked separately. They would not mix at all, because that, too, was normal for them all.

At roll-call the next morning the British POWs realised that the sergeant in charge of the whole camp – who had previously had charge of the Dutch camp party only – spoke English, of a kind, and he obviously enjoyed displaying that skill. The Japanese had discovered that the sacks of food carried by the Dutch had been pilfered. Instead of using care to pilfer without damaging the hessian sacking, they had pilfered crudely. Instead of taking only a reasonable quantity from each and every sack, they stole a lot from one sack of sugar and a lot from one sack of fish. They had been POWs almost as long as the Brits but had not yet become professionals!

The sergeant set about enjoying the occasion immensely. He kept the British on parade so that he had an audience before whom he could act, an audience who would surely appreciate his linguistic skills, and his humour. His performance went thus: 'Some Dutch gentlemen, who is not gentlemen, steal sugar and fish from Japanese. That gentlemen must stand forward.' When no one responded to his invitation, he said, 'Perhaps all Dutch soldier not gentlemen. Perhaps I slap all non-gentlemen's face. Perhaps I also bash the non-gentlemen's sergeant major.' He then set about his promised face slapping performance, and followed it with a few swings at the unfortunate sergeant major.

Of course, he had not yet finished displaying his command of English. He made a speech which indicated that he, and many other Japanese in charge of POWs, had all had a similar education in terms of learning English. He compared Australian, British and Dutch POWs, proclaiming, 'Australia soldier, plenty work, no brains — English soldier, plenty brains, no work — Dutch soldier, no brains, no work, no bruddy gentlemens.' But of course he was wrong, not just in his use of the language, but in detail as well. The Aussies did have brains – they had showed the Brits the ropes during the early days of captivity at River Valley Road camp. And with a little more time, the Dutch, too, would use their brains and become expert at pilfering, and the Japanese would not then have cause to think they were not gentlemen!

The British party constructed two shelters from bamboo and heavily leafed tree branches – and prayed that it would not rain. They shared the pig with the Dutch, but kept that fact from the Japanese. The chickens, boiled with the rice for the evening meal, could just be tasted. There was some urgency to consume the sugar and fish to reduce the chances of being found out, but the pork was made to last in the stockpot for a few days.

They were in very hilly country in Southern Burma, near Myitta, about thirty-five miles from Tavoy. Their road would soon meet an existing road leading to Myitta and Tavoy, and then their task would, hopefully, be over. Theirs was the most westerly POW camp on that road, but there was a Japanese camp west of them, thought to be entrusted with control of the project. The task the men had was to widen the track already there, and to bridge the many gullies which interrupted the track, because gullies abounded in those hills. The gullies were dry but would clearly carry swiftly falling water during the monsoon rains, which were just three months away. They were required to make sturdy bridges, well clear of the waters which would gush down the gullies. The work, whether widening the track by cutting back into the side of the hill or building bridges, was heavy. But the worst aspect was that it was 'Speedo' time again.

One evening, well after dark, a guard – obviously the most junior one in the camp – was required by his seniors to visit the Japanese camp about four miles to the west of them, to collect, or deliver, a document. The camps were linked by field telephone and the request came from the other camp. The only problem for the junior Japanese soldier – who had been appointed courier by his seniors – was that he was terrified. His seniors had agreed that he could take a British POW as an escort, but had not designated who it was to be. The soldier asked, almost pleaded, for a volunteer, obviously not wanting a pressed man who might add to his fears and hazards, but none would volunteer. The guard had become nearly frantic – it was urgent, he had to leave soon – but still no one stepped forward. Archie Gibson could not stand the tension any longer, and the guard smiled happily when Archie said simply, 'OK. I go.'

The guard's fear was rational and easily understood. It was a dark night and the track through the jungle was in hilly country. Gullies had to be crossed, and some were still unbridged. The possibility of meeting a tiger or bear was remote during the day, but it seemed a much less remote possibility to anyone having to walk that track on a very dark night. An accident, perhaps a broken leg, could be disastrous for a man out there on his own. It was likely that many in the camp would also have been very unhappy to be made to go on that same walk in darkness and alone.

The two set out, the guard with a flaming torch which incorporated coconut oil, and Archie with an unlit torch in reserve. Nearly four hours later they returned and Archie told his friends about the trip. The guard had chatted away loudly and demanded of Archie that he too should do his fair share of talking loudly. At the destination he had been given some food to eat outside the camp kitchen, whilst the guard ate and chatted with cronies inside. Then it was time to return and he was again required to talk loudly all the way back. His reward when the trip was completed had been a pint of peanuts from the guard, and from his friends the observation that since the escort had to be a chatterbox, he had been ideally suited for the walk.

Just a few days later the road was deemed to be completed and the men were told they would soon have to start the trek back to Wampo West. The Japanese increased the men's rations and gave them some sugar and sea-weed as well. The senior guards went ahead of the others, leaving the men to the mercies of humble privates.

The day before they were due to march Ron developed malaria. On the morning of the march his temperature raged and the medical orderly told the guards he could neither march nor be carried. The orderly had to resist a guard who wanted to dip Ron in the river to reduce his temperature. Finally it was agreed that a guard, the orderly and the patient would remain behind for three days. The rest would leave at once.

In terms of distance, Wampo was a four or five day march away and there was no inclination to rush. It was a more pleasant trek than any previously experienced and the men were also glad to be getting away from the region which they feared might soon become infested with retreating enemy soldiers. They spent the first night at the site of the former Dutch camp, and set off again early the next morning before the sun emerged over the hills east of them. By the evening they were beside a wide river, their senior guards were there in tents, and the men were told to rest there to await the arrival of Ron and the orderly two or three days later.

The men slept in the open, in a bamboo forest adjacent to the river and bordering the jungle. Never before had they experienced so many mosquitoes – it was much worse than the infestation in the Death Valley camp which they had experienced during the march into the jungle to build the railway twenty-eight months earlier. Mosquitoes abounded in all areas where massive bamboo grew because water was always trapped in broken canes, particularly if the canes were wide, and they were ample breeding pools for mosquitoes. The men spent the evening beside a smoking fire, as near the smoke as they could tolerate, to avoid the worst of the infestation. And later they hid under their hessian blankets, as best they could, trying to shield themselves from the tormenting insects, but with only very limited success because the blankets were small.

The performance was repeated the next evening and night and they looked forward to the time when they could leave that mosquito ridden place. Ron, the medical orderly and the remaining guard arrived on the third evening, so they were to resume their trek to Wampo the next morning. That transit camp would close and be reclaimed by the jungle. The guards gave them a pig and several pounds of soya beans, so they were to feast that night, all thirty-one of them.

And feast they did. They ate a thick stew of cubed pork and

soya beans and nothing else. And when they finished their giant helping, they went back for more. There was plenty and they could not pack any surplus to take away with them, so all ate greedily. And in the morning, those who were gluttons – and most were – had it for breakfast as well. Pork, beans and no rice! They had not expected to feast like that until the war ended.

Then they commenced the third leg of their trek to Wampo. The wide river was crossed on a large raft in a single trip; the party hauled themselves across by pulling on a steel cable suspended across the river. They were still in Burma, still in very hilly terrain, and still in pairs which shared a load suspended from a bamboo pole. Ron and Ian were again paired together, and after several miles Ian was in some difficulty. On those treks he had always struggled more than just a little because his legs and ankles were less strong than they should have been. But now he also had pains in his stomach and chest, was perspiring heavily, felt ill and struggled to remain on his feet. Ron took the back end of the pole because they were on an uphill gradient, and urged him to keep going. 'Just stay on your feet,' he said, 'and I'll push.' But by then Ian was starting to stagger. The medical orderly, who had kept a watching brief, asked the guard to stop the march. The guard had been aware of the slowness of the pair, his impatient shouting at them had progressively become more insistent, but now he accepted that Ian was ill. Their load was redistributed among all the other pairs, with some of it retained for Ron to carry on his own. The guard ordered Ian and the medical orderly – who was never paired on those treks because he had to be available for incidents such as this – to recommence the trek immediately, whilst the rest of the party had a rest break. And he further ordered that the two should not have any more rest breaks that day, but should keep going all the time so that they would not delay progress.

The two set off. The orderly kept Ian on the inside of the track so that he would not stagger off the edge and fall down the hill, because he had become quite dizzy and was tending to stagger. They were near to the top of the hill at the time Ian had been relieved of his carrying duties, had reached the top since then and were on a downward gradient when Ian was near to collapse. Then he was sick. He brought up all the pork and beans he had eaten for breakfast, then all he had eaten the previous night, which in total was quite a bit. He immediately began to feel much better, though drained and weak. He was still just a few feet away from the vomited mess, because the orderly insisted that he should rest. Ian, who had not realised earlier that it was only his gluttony which was the cause of his trouble, was relieved to discover that he was not really ill, and favoured moving off straight away, but was restrained by the orderly and made to lie down. He did not know that he was still pale and weak.

The party behind emerged from a bend in the road and were relieved when they neared the two seated on the ground, saw the mess and realised the cause of Ian's problem. The guard was excited; pointing at Ian and the mess he shouted in triumphant accusation, '*Tuc-san bishi, tuc-san bishi.*' But Ian hardly needed to be told that he had eaten 'too much pig, too much pig'.

They insisted that he remain there with the orderly whilst they continued the trek. The camp at which they were all to spend the night was at the foot of the hill they were trekking down, less than two miles away. They would dump their loads there and return with a stretcher. In due course, Ron, Archie and two others returned with a real stretcher, and he was carried all the way to the camp.

Weeks earlier the area in which that camp was situated had been christened 'Bondi', because it reminded the men of a wide shingle strewn beach. The shingles were, of course, an area of scree which had originated from the hill. When the party had passed through on the outward journey, the site was occupied by Thais, a mere three huts on stilts. But the Thais were not there any longer, though their huts remained. There were about one hundred POWs in the tented camp. Two of the stilted huts were occupied by Japanese and the third was deemed to be a first aid post.

Ian was deposited in the first aid hut because the MO had seen him being carried in, and wanted to see the casualty. The orderly stayed to await the MO, whom Ian recognised immediately. He was Major Black who had prescribed emetine for his dysentery about fourteen months earlier – and the MO had some recollection of Ian, too, and asked where they had met before. The orderly told the MO about the pork and beans and the march. The MO remained surprisingly patient. He smiled and remarked that he was glad his services were not really required, and that Ian would be OK by the next morning.

They spent the day at that camp doing nothing in particular. Ian was puzzled because a cluster of banana trees on the outskirts had bananas on them. What was wrong with the men in the camp, he wondered. Did they not recognise bananas? A nearby troupe of monkeys had not plundered them either, it was strange. Then he pushed over a tree with fruit which seemed ripe and ready for eating. He discovered they were wild bananas, their skins packed to capacity with seeds, each the size of a small pea, leaving room only for a sticky substance wrapped around each seed. They had a banana smell – so he tasted with his tongue – but they were tasteless, so he gave up. Then he wondered why it was that he knew of no other POW who was so ready to sample fruits or berries or young shoots from plants in the jungle – and concluded that it was probably because he had less wisdom than anyone else.

The following morning the trek re-started. There were no

casualties and they were back in terrain which was mostly flat; good progress was made. By the evening they had arrived at a camp of several tents, occupied by only two Japanese. The surrounding area was scrub land for as far as the eye could see, and there was a small stream a hundred yards away.

Shortly after midnight the men were awakened by yelling Japanese. There was a bush fire raging to the east of the camp across a wide front and advancing towards the camp. It was half a mile away but a stiff breeze was behind it and the camp was in some danger. The panic-stricken guards required them to tackle the blaze.

Armed with small branches torn from shrubs, and shovels, they ran to the face of the fire and set about trying to beat it out. The fire was on a wide front, presenting a danger that men could be encircled. Fortunately, among the men was at least one who knew how the task should be tackled. When the guards realised that they could not beat out the fire, they gave him a hearing. They agreed to his plan to retreat to the stream – which was between the fire and the camp – and then start small controlled fires from the edge of the stream and advancing towards the fire. The idea was to create a fire break of burnt out terrain between the stream and the fire.

That was achieved but the men still had to extinguish small fresh fires started by sparks blown across the fire break, because the vegetation was dry and sparks were easily ignited into flames. That particular threat was over when the wide front of the fire was broken by the fire break, and the fire remained only on the sides.

The men then manned the side areas to prevent the fire from encroaching sideways into the camp area, from north or south. When the fire had passed on both sides of the camp, they started more controlled fires to the west of the camp, so that the camp was then surrounded completely by burnt out terrain. About three hours after being called out the men returned to their interrupted sleep. Later they heard thundering of hooves and wondered what animals were stampeding.

In the morning it was agreed that the stampede was probably that of a herd of elephants, but no one knew if there were wild elephants in that region of Thailand.

They set off early again the next morning and at mid-day recognised the pass they trekked through. It was the one in which the stray bull had caused all that excitement. Then they passed the site of their former Christmas camp. The jungle was reclaiming it. In the evening they stopped at a camp they knew to be five or six miles from Wampo West, and were to rest there for the night.

Captain Pitt, the MO, was temporarily in this camp and was to return to Wampo the next day. He was pleased to see those men, but told them they were in a worse state than their morale suggested, and that he would endeavour to secure their early return to Tamuang, their base camp. He confirmed the story of the killing of a POW by a drunken Japanese warrant officer shortly after the men had left that camp in December.

The next morning they set off on the final leg of the trek back to Wampo West. On the way they passed men going in the opposite direction, each weighed down by a sack of rice on his shoulders. They were unable to stop for a chat!

The party arrived at Wampo West and Captain Pitt examined them all that afternoon. He confirmed his view that all should return to Tamuang as soon as possible, and said he would press the Japanese. He understood their joy that they were back in a location from which they could be transported to comparative civilisation, but urged them to avoid laughter and jollity in the sight of Japanese. And if Japanese were around they should droop their shoulders and wear a hang-dog look. He suggested, too, that all had squitters and should stick to that story. He warned that if they remained there they would be used as beasts of burden, to carry sacks of rice along the mule track they had just made, because it was a supply route for Japanese forces in Burma – and he had not seen any four-legged mules in the vicinity.

But there was a small but important matter the men had to attend to before complying with the MO's advice. Important, because it related to a good meal. The Japanese had again been careless with their pigs, having let one escape in this camp too, several days earlier. Tom, who had seen the men arrive, quickly invited them to catch the pig for themselves. He suggested they fan out wide in the surrounding jungle and drive the pig towards the river bank. All the men needed was to have a semi-circle of determined and alert men, and the pig would be in the bag. Or so they thought.

They were successful in closing in on the pig, but could not catch and hold it, so they drove it into the river. Unfortunately for Ian he was nearest the river's edge when the animal plunged into the water, and in moments of great excitement he was prone to forget that he was a very poor swimmer, and also to overlook that he still had his boots on. So he plunged in after the pig which was being carried by the current towards mid-stream.

He was in the water only a minute or two before he realised there was no chance whatever that he could catch up with the pig, let alone catch it. He had realised, too, that he was wearing his boots and was further from the bank then was likely to be good for him – the current having carried him out. Ron and the others yelled to him to return, but he heard them only after he had turned to return. He made the bank without help, but it had been a struggle, and he knew he had been foolish.

A good swimmer had plunged in when he realised that the pig

was a faster swimmer than Ian, and they passed each other going in opposite directions. He brought the pig back successfully.

Ian was cross with himself for having been so foolhardy. Twenty-seven months earlier he had plunged in from the river bank exactly opposite, to collect fish from the dynamited river, and had then been in grave danger of drowning. Would he never learn?

The pig went to the cookhouse for all the POWs in camp, but the small party of men who caught it did not mind, they had enjoyed the hunt. Now they were free to take Captain Pitt's advice about being stricken with squitters.

At roll-call the next morning the Japanese commandant explained to them their work for the future. They would each carry a sack of rice to a dump in the next camp; in due course there would be more men to carry rice, and it would be carried from dump to dump all along the track they had made. He thanked them for helping the Emperor by making the road; they could start carrying immediately.

A guard supervised whilst a sack was slung onto each man's shoulder and rear neck. As each was loaded he set off because there was no point in hanging about with that burden. The men were unescorted, and there would be no one to reload a sack were it to be dropped or jettisoned. Ridiculous though it seemed, the men had to carry a sack of rice – which probably weighed more than a hundredweight – some five miles or so, without a break. The thought of it was more than enough to confirm in each man's mind that he had chronic squitters.

The men learned within a few minutes that a coolie trot was best. So they trotted on and on. When a trot became wobbly, the man would find a suitable roadside tree to lean against, whilst still retaining the sack on his shoulder. After a truly short break he would re-start his trot. It was imperative that the sack remained on their shoulders, because in their fatigued state they would not have the strength to re-load it if it fell off. The trip took about an hour and a half, on average. Then the men rested and returned to Wampo West in the afternoon.

The beast of burden job was a horrendous task for most men. Those like Preston, who were built like tanks and had enormous strength, almost took the task in their stride, but they were exceptional. All the others struggled, but none more than Ian, whose legs were so wobbly he leaned against more trees than anyone else. Afterwards he tried to joke about propping up more trees than anyone else, but he knew there was no funny side.

Being beasts of burden was telling on the men quite a bit. They had been at it for several days and even Preston had wilted. Captain Pitt saw them daily and told them that the commandant had agreed to their return soon, but he warned that it was not in the bag yet and they needed to look sick and miserable at all times. Perhaps he had not realised that many of them were no longer acting. Then he told them the commandant had agreed to put them on the first train to pass through Wampo from the north. That would be after darkness on any future day, so the men should hold themselves in readiness every evening, and should continue to look ill. Meanwhile they continued to carry those sacks of rice.

At dawn one day the RAF visited Wampo, flew low over the 'station' and rained bombs. The men in Wampo West could see the planes about six hundred yards away, and flattened themselves in the open rainwater drain below the roof edge of each hut. All of them did that except for the unhappy loner. He sprinted away and ran down the road out of view and, in Archie's words, 'Was halfway to Bondi before we were even in the drain' – which was a remarkable achievement by a man whose bad knees had excused him from all heavy work, including carrying his share of loads each time the men had trekked to another camp.

Since some of the planes had flown above the river and followed its course south, and seconds later explosions were heard from a southerly direction, it was thought the viaduct at Wampo South had also been targeted. The men realised the raid could well delay their return to Tamuang.

But that evening, before dusk, they were taken across the river by barge and walked to Wampo 'station' to await a train, which was likely to arrive later. Captain Pitt accompanied them. They saw that the planes had hit their target, a row of wagons hidden in a jungle siding well away from the main track. They had been concealed under branches and camouflage netting, but evidently not well enough. Some thought their location had probably been transmitted to the forces in Burma by men behind enemy lines.

After half an hour or so, the commandant arrived on the scene and said the train was imminent. Soon they heard the noise of its approach and saw its smoke. The train stopped just to collect the men, and they were told to climb onto the wagon roofs, and to do it speedo. They climbed aboard with such speed and agility that the commandant was upset and remonstrated with Captain Pitt about the men's fitness. But the train pulled away with all the men aboard. Later they regretted that they had unthinkingly let Captain Pitt down and knew that, as a consequence, he was less likely to be able to influence the commandant in the future. The men were *en route* for Tamuang.

CHAPTER 7

Tamuang, Bangkok, Takli, and Freedom

THE JOURNEY BACK TO TAMUANG was largely a repeat of the outgoing one made some three months earlier. Again they clung to one another and also had a plane spotting strategy, but there were differences – sparks were a much smaller problem. The crossing over the viaduct at Wampo South was even more worrying than before because that was probably the first train to travel on it since that morning, and the men had thought the RAF had targeted it also. They worried lest the structure had been damaged. The journey back was much quicker than the outgoing one had been; possibly the train had a lighter load, probably there were more downhill gradients.

They arrived at Tamuang station and marched to the camp in the early hours of the morning. Though escorted, they were refused admission by the sentry at the gate because he had not been told to expect them. He used his telephone and a sergeant arrived; the sentry's face was slapped, then the men were admitted and taken to an empty hut to bed down for the rest of the night.

In the morning they were seen by Captain Pavillard, who was relieved to see them. He had been warned by the Japanese to expect sick men, and was pleased to discover that the Japanese were somewhat mistaken.

The returning men learned that Charlie Letts had been caught whilst returning to camp one night. The Japanese had found him at the bottom of the trench — it was said that his bamboo pole had broken during his vault back. There was much confusion and rumour about what punishment the Japanese had inflicted upon him, but the men were reassured by senior POWs that he had not been executed. Somehow he escaped very serious punishment.

The Japanese planned to send men to many working camps all over Thailand. All, including those who had just returned, knew they were vulnerable and could be drafted any day. Again Ron looked forward to leaving the base camp as soon as possible. Perhaps the trench surrounding the perimeter was a good enough reason for men to want to be sent elsewhere, but Ian lacked confidence in his physical fitness for heavy work and was apprehensive about the nature of any work lying in store for him on a future project.

It was early in April 1945 when a party of about three hundred, including Ian and his brother, left Tamuang after dark one evening for an unknown destination. They boarded a train at Tamuang station, again travelling on the roofs of wagons, and were off. But after only half an hour or so, the train stopped for the engine to be uncoupled and driven off on another track, to pull other wagons. The men were required to push the engineless train from there on – to Bangkok, it was learned. They were happy enough that the RAF was obviously doing a very good job at destroying rolling-stock, and had no great difficulty in carrying out the Japanese orders, which were: 'All men push.'

So push they did. On downhill gradients some ran after the train whilst others clung on to whatever bits of the rear trucks they could, lifted their feet off the track and became free riders – remarkably, no one was seriously injured. The journey had started soon after dark, but it was well into the next day before they finally arrived in Bangkok. Surprisingly, the civilians did not regard it as strange that the train had no engine and had to be pushed.

Obviously, too, many other POWs had passed their way, because they did not give the men a second look.

They were walked through the streets to the river-front, where they bunked down in a large empty warehouse built from steel girders and galvanised iron sheets. The building had obviously been a target – at the very least a machine-gun target – for raiding planes; its roof and walls bore considerable evidence of that. No one seemed to know how long they would remain there, or where they were going, but for the men it was all a pleasant change. They whiled away the time in relaxed viewing of river traffic, and when the guards were absent were able to make hurried purchases from boat traders. At other times, when the air raid sirens sounded, they made hurried exits from the warehouse, and ran as fast as they could, hearts pounding, to trenches dug on waste ground downstream. On these flights from the warehouse, they ran through streets alongside Thais, all urgently putting as much distance between themselves and the warehouse as possible.

They stayed there for nearly a week, a pleasant week it was, too, in comparison with the standards they had come to expect as being their unavoidable lot. Then they were marched off to the station to board a train of open trucks. The men sat on the floors, there was no serious overcrowding and the views of paddy fields and small villages were there for all to see. But they did not know where they were headed for, nor what lay in store for them.

The train stopped at three stations which were reminiscent of the shanty towns depicted in Westerns. Locals lined the track to view the POWs, some to greet them with friendly smiles and friendly acts. It appeared they might never have seen white men before, and at all three stops the men were the centre of much attention. Blue eyes seemed enough of a surprise to the Thais, but men with really fair hair, or more extravagantly, red hair, seemed to cause the most curious delight.

Much warmth was displayed towards them at these stops, and it seemed that many Thais were trying to convey a message. But if they were, it was lost because of the language problem. Certainly the guards were very much on edge, unable to curb the curiosity and excitement, or to stop the Thais in their efforts to communicate with the POWs. In particular, the guards showed most concern about objects being thrown to the men, objecting even to the throwing of tangerines. It was thought the real concern of the guards was that written messages might also be thrown.

At the last of the stops a Thai said, more than once, 'Germany finish,' but was unable to say more than just that, despite having opportunities to do so. It seemed as though he had hastily learned just those two words; it was apparent that he had an insistent message to convey, but could not be precise. Those who heard him thought he probably meant Germany was taking a beating and that he was forecasting that Germany had no chance of winning the war. But they also felt, perhaps, that that was the very least he was saying. Maybe, just maybe, the Germans had sued for peace, maybe the European war was over.

But none dared believe, or even dwell on, those optimistic possibilities, because they feared the devastating blow to their morale if that optimism later proved to be wrong. They were conditioned to knowing and remembering that they had been deceived by rumours right from the earliest days of their captivity, and had long since been conditioned to disbelieve anything told them, until there was overwhelming reason to believe. That was an inevitable consequence of being shut off from the world for already more than three years, without a supply of first-hand news which they could switch on and listen to, or read in a newspaper. There was so much they wanted to believe, but none dared.

Finally the train stopped near Takli, a very small town near the centre of Thailand. They were marched into a camp which had the kind of huts POWs had become used to, but there was evidence of the whole place having been sprayed from the air with machine-guns. The camp was about a mile from an aircraft landing strip, a small one, surrounded by hills; perhaps it was only suitable for fighter aircraft. Their task was to re-surface the strip, using gravel which was conveniently available in adjoining gravel beds.

They commenced work the next day, but as well as three cooks, four others remained in camp to dig a well because there was no natural source of water available. Meanwhile a water wagon supplied the camp. On day four, after the well was thirty feet deep and still dry, a water diviner stepped forward; the guards were amused but agreed to let the man show them where the well should be. So the man divined and the incredulous guards looked on as his twig convulsed in a spasm of energy, and he said, 'Dig here,' pointing to the ground at his feet.

They dug there and at less than twenty feet struck muddy soup. A few more feet down and there was genuine water, though milky in appearance. But the water wagon continued to call daily to supply the guards with better quality stuff, while the men used the milky well water to cook with and to drink. After a mere three days the men began to have difficulties with their kidneys. By the fifth day none could pee and all had severe kidney and other pains. None could possibly work.

A Japanese medical officer examined some men and from thereon the water wagon provided water for the entire camp. But it was several days later before the men recovered enough to re-start work on the landing strip, and some continued to have kidney pains.

Each morning after the camp guards had completed the roll-call formalities, men from a Japanese engineering regiment arrived in camp to march them to the airstrip. There, equipped with shovels and bamboo stretchers, pairs of men dug up gravel and carried it to fill dips in the airstrip. One man was always allowed to be 'tea-boy', and they took turns for that easy job. The tea-boy simply collected water from the gravel pit and boiled it for the men to drink during rest periods. Possibly that water had a lot to do with continuing kidney pains. But it was that, or nothing. And they had to drink to avoid dehydration in the extreme heat on that job, from which it was impossible to take refuge from the sun.

There was a steam-roller, but it did not work – so men pulled it up and down the strip with the aid of stout ropes. And some had to push it because there was not enough rope. During their time as POWs they had heard the call 'All men push,' on all kinds of occasions. They had pushed lorries in Singapore because they had no petrol, and sometimes because they had no engines. They had pushed lorries on the road outside Tamuang camp for mile after mile, because they had broken down. They had pushed barges off sand banks on the Kwai when they were in railway camps. They had pushed trains without engines, one to Bangkok. Now it was a steam-roller.

Apart from the tea-boy, all had a tough day every day, and the sun, from which there was no shade at all, was fierce and merciless. But worse was to come, even for the tea-boy. They were told of the requirement to dig a trench three metres wide and deep, around the camp perimeter. And that was to be done after the normal workday on the strip. Fortunately, the monsoons started after the trench had progressed only thirty yards, filling it with water. It became impossible to continue digging because, even at surface level, water immediately filled the hole caused by the removal of each spadeful of soil. The Japanese had to make do with only their machine-guns at the four corners of the bamboo fenced camp.

But there was also cheerful news. Large aircraft could be heard flying over most nights, and they seemed to be unopposed. Leaflets had been dropped – some fell in camp – with Japanese characters and sketches showing Japan being bombed by planes operating from aircraft carriers. On their march to the airstrip each morning one or two young Thai men showed up to repeat their brief news almost every day. But they had changed their oft repeated phrase from 'Germany finish' to 'Germany kaput', which seemed a more powerful message. But none in camp felt certain that hostilities in Europe had ended.

One day, after a leaflet raid the previous night, a guard approached a group of men during a rest break. He asked, 'Englando aeroplane, four engines. How many man inside?' Drum Major Harris leapt in quickly to ensure that he alone answered. 'Three hundred and four,' he said, then wrote down the number in the dust with his finger, so that there could be no misunderstanding. He was a quick-witted man with a tremendous sense of humour and fun, huge eyes and a bristling moustache, all three of which he used expressively. He had made monkeys of guards before, and intended to do so again – and he had an audience of his comrades to perform in front of, so was in his element.

'Three hundred and four,' mused the guard in Japanese. 'Whaa,' he said shaking his head in amazement as he checked the number the Drum Major had written in the dust. Then he brightened a little and demanded, 'How? How?'

The Drum Major did not delay his answer, and his audience was anxious because his arithmetic seemed as though it was likely to be very wrong. It seemed to them he would be hopelessly short of his three hundred and four target. And, worse still, the guard was slowing him down to record the details in the dust. The Drum Major said the planes were crewed by: 6 drivers – and with his hands indicated a steering action; 6 radio men – and by actions illustrated them; 50 throw-out-bombs men, illustrated by actions; 30 machine-gun-men, illustrated, and with appropriate noises; 10

look-see men, illustrated with imaginary binoculars; 4 tea-boys; 4 men sick; 2 doctors; 40 men look-see today, come-back tomorrow.

The guard did his sums, then triumphantly and threateningly demanded, 'More one hundred and fifty men where?' As though he was surprised to be asked, Harris said in throw-away fashion, 'Half-time, all men changey-changey.'

All present knew the art of keeping a straight face and none had betrayed any sign of surprise or even serious interest, and certainly not one of amusement. The guard went away and was quiet and subdued for the rest of the day.

He came back to the same group at the lunch break the next day and defiantly proclaimed the wonders of Japanese military might. 'Nippon number one,' he declared defiantly. 'Nippon army number one, Nippon ship number one, Nippon aeroplane number one.' The men were noncommittal, knowing that if they disagreed he would bash them, and if they listened he might pass round his cigarettes. 'Nippon got new number one aeroplane,' he said. 'Nippon new aeroplane, full of bomb, fly very high. World turn round, Americano underneath, Nippon aeroplane drop bomb, boom, boom boom. World turn round more, Englando underneath, Nippon aeroplane drop more bomb, boom, boom, boom. World turn round more, Nippon underneath, aeroplane go down, take more bomb, same again all time.'

The men looked unconcerned, but showed no disbelief. The Drum Major asked him, 'Nippon soldier, you know how world turn round?' The guard did not, '*Nai, nai*,' he said, almost inquiringly. Harris enlightened him with words, and with figures written in the dust. 'One thousand million English America boy soldier, all training to be man soldier, they all push.'

The guard was baffled, even demoralised. He slunk away. And the men quickly worked out what had probably happened. They guessed that when he had returned to his cronies the previous evening and told them about the air crew of three hundred and four, they had recognised the leg-pull, and told him about that wonder aircraft – he had swallowed that as well. The POWs wished they could be there to see the reaction that evening when the guard told the tale of woe about all those trainee soldiers the Allies had.

Marching out to work one morning the men were furtively, yet insistently, told by a young Thai, 'War finish. You come with me.' They heard him, but did not believe him. Ian was tea-boy that day, so was on his own and without a guard in sight, but he knew of the possibility that a guard was secretly watching. The same Thai, partly concealed as he squatted in the long grass, called quietly to him, 'War finish. You come. Quick please.' Ian knew what he was saying, but could not believe him. One problem was that there was a reward for any civilian who handed in an escaped POW – all were aware of that. But the main problem was that all of them were still conditioned to disbelief, unless there was positive proof. And there was none of that.

That evening a man in camp produced a note, tied to a stone and signed by a Major somebody, informing the camp that the war was over but they should sit tight and wait. The poor fellow who found the note was disbelieved and ridiculed by all. In the end it was accepted that he had truly found the note, but it was thought that some clown in camp had dropped it for him to find. And he was also persuaded that that was what had happened.

The next day, and on subsequent days, the men were taken out to work just as usual, and the Thai no longer appeared to tell them the war was ended. They really had no substantial reason to think the war was over.

Then one morning, after the usual roll-call by the camp guards, the engineer guards failed to arrive to march them to the airstrip. The men sat on the ground, still in lines, and waited. After some twenty minutes a Japanese officer arrived and said there would be no work that day. Exactly the same thing happened the next morning, and the men became very anxious. Only two possibilities occurred to them. The more attractive one was that the airstrip was deemed to be completed and the men were about to be moved urgently to another project. The other possibility was that the men were being kept in camp in preparation for a massacre. They chose to believe the more pleasant of the alternatives, but were worried.

The third morning was a repetition of the two preceding ones, but the officer also told them they could have a camp concert in the evening. They spent the day collecting fuel for the two campfires they would have that evening, one on each side of the 'stage'. The concert started soon after dark and the men tried to overlook the worries they had. Most knew they would be defenceless against machine-guns, and that they were unable to affect the course of events.

They started with community singing, and their concert was well under way when there was a commotion at the back, and two men appeared and strode to the front. They were dressed in green uniforms, one with a strange-looking sub-machine gun, both with parachute emblems on their shirts, neither with any badge of rank. Since the men did not know that the European war was over, nor that the Japanese war was over, had never seen sten guns, nor British troops in green uniforms, nor British troops without badges of rank, nor knew about the formation of the parachute regiment, but did know about German parachutists, those who thought the two men approaching were 'German bastards' who should go home, should be forgiven.

The officer, who was the Major 'somebody', spoke, and then the men were positively able to believe the war was indeed over. He told them so with his opening words, and said that he had tried to inform the camp earlier but his efforts had failed. He told them it had been necessary for all the Japanese in the area to be told of their defeat before the two paratroopers could show themselves. During the wait he had been in touch with the senior Japanese in the vicinity, and the Thai mayor of the town, and had ensured the safety of the POWs.

He explained that the guards had evacuated their quarters in the camp as soon as the concert had started. Some men then rushed to the guards' hut to look for any who might still be there, but returned empty-handed. He told them the Allies were aware of the enemy's plan to massacre POWs if the territory on which they were held was invaded. Therefore, soldiers like himself had shadowed POW camps for weeks – with the help of underground armies – to report back on the enemy strength in the regions, and the fitness of the POWs to shoulder arms, so that when the invasion took place sufficient forces and arms would be dropped to protect POW camps. He told them the invasion of Thailand and Malaya had been near but was deferred when Japanese surrender was imminent. He told them of the atom bombing of the two Japanese cities.

He said the Allies were aware of what had taken place on the railway, that there would be war crime trials and that every POW would be invited to make statements about crimes and to name those responsible, by their proper names or by nicknames. Convicted war criminals would be properly punished, and if they were murderers, then they would be hanged. He assured the men that their comrades who had died would be avenged, but it depended on each of the men to furnish proper evidence of the crimes of which they had first hand evidence.

He said planes would fly over in the morning to drop food, medical supplies, and a MO because he knew there was not one in camp. He said that, provided the airstrip was suitable for Dakotas, they would all be flown to Rangoon. He explained that a Dakota would land the next morning to conduct take-off trials with varying quantities of sandbags. If the airstrip was unsuitable, they would be taken to a suitable airfield and flown from there. He reassured them that they would not be required to march, that whatever the eventuality, they would be conveyed. Their marching, trekking days were over.

He said that political decisions to demobilise them immediately upon their return to Britain, and to speed that return, had already been taken. He told them that Lord Mountbatten had promised comfortable conditions in ships taking them home. The men were numbed by the hurricane of good tidings with which they had so suddenly been confronted. In a kind of dazed state, they shook every hand they could. They were thankful for survival, congratulated one another. Some said stupid things like, 'We're men, if we weren't we could not have survived,' which displeased those who knew that much better men than themselves had died, and who knew that survival had, to a very great extent, been decided by fortune.

They sang the National Anthem and every patriotic song they knew, they wandered around, sat down, stood up, did not know what to do next. They were filled with a cocktail of stark memories and powerful emotions. They, who were all grateful to have survived, briefly overlooked the tribulations they had personally endured, and thought of their particular friends and close comrades who had died, and why and how. They were joyful that deliverance had come, but were sad, angry, guilty that their friends had died. And thousands of their comrades whom they did not personally know, but comrades nevertheless, had also died. The tears flowing freely from many eyes were not just tears of joy and relief, but tears for their lost friends. And many were to remain on the edge of tears for days and days to come.

It was a strange night that followed that remarkable evening.

Men, though tired by the lateness of the hour and by the volume and power of the many emotions which surrounded and confronted them, stayed awake just to lengthen and hang on to that wonderful day. And when they could no longer stay awake, they could only sleep fitfully, unable to relax sufficiently to have more than a quick doze. And many, including Ian, awakened two, three or even more times, and on each occasion thought they had just had the most wonderful dream that the war was over. Then, confused and anxious, they would ask some other man who was also awake, if it was only a dream or if that day had really happened. Between them they logically came to the right conclusion, because both would not have dreamed the identical details. After he had awakened for the second time believing it was only a complicated and very confusing dream, Ian stayed awake for the remainder of the night to ensure that he did not again, however briefly, suffer the dreadful misery of thinking the events of that day were only a dream. And whilst awake he peacefully savoured the joy of that wonderful day over and over again. And even the sadness and guilt about having lost good friends did not reduce his joy; those emotions were not buried or suppressed or ignored, they lived alongside the magnificent joy of that day. He knew that the three and a half years of captivity by the Japanese would impact on his mind and soul for the rest of his life.

And in the morning their joy was just as great, and savoured all over again. The Dakota landed to deliver a Medical Officer, and to commence take-off trials. Within hours, the RAF declared that the strip was OK for take-off with loads of up to twenty men at a time.

The arrival of the MO was critical for one man, Bert, who was in a coma with black water fever. That illness had been generally fatal in POW camps because proper medication was not available. In Takli, not only was there not proper medication, there had not even been a MO. But the situation had changed just in time to save Bert's life. The MO was confident Bert would recover and the optimistic prognosis spread quickly, and the relief and happiness of the men was intense.

Before mid-day a Mitchell bomber flew low over the camp, and with dipped wings greeted the men. All had been told to keep away from the parade ground and that side of the camp, so that supplies could be dropped. But the men were ecstatic, concerned only to show the crew – some of whom were seen waving through an open doorway – how wonderfully joyous they were. The plane turned and made a second pass, but the crew still could not drop the supplies because the parade ground was also the best vantage point from which the men were determined to stand, wave and cheer – to see the plane and to be seen in their great happiness. A crew member with a hand-held camera was seen photographing the scene below.

The third pass was nearer the edge of the camp. Bomb doors opened and canisters were released; at the same time crates, with parachutes attached, were shoved out of the open doorway. No one in camp was injured, but the men had expected a parachute drop only – had they known that canisters, without parachutes, were to be dropped, they would have retreated from the parade ground earlier. And that was what they did on subsequent days.

A jeep was delivered by the Dakota for camp use. Daily drops of supplies ensured that no more hopeless rice need be eaten, and there were clothes for the men, too. Some men, perhaps most, took their new clothing to the village to trade for chickens. They were content to remain in their jap-happies, which were cool and easy to wash, and were also eager to taste chicken again. And they also saw no point in allowing lice a foothold in the clothes they would wear when they were returned to civilisation. By day three Bert was conscious again, weak but very cheerful. It was planned to fly him to Rangoon as soon as he was strong enough. The sick were to be flown out first, and lots would be drawn to settle the sequence of departure for the rest. The total evacuation might take many days because the monsoons were not yet over, and the rate of departures was very much constrained by the weather. There were days when aircraft could neither land or take-off because of the water-logged airstrip.

Colonel Lilly arrived in camp, escorted by Sergeant Takeda, who had been the senior Japanese NCO in Wampo. He was a decent fellow against whom no one had a grudge. The brave and tireless Colonel had felt a responsibility to visit every POW camp in Thailand, to ensure that all of them were accounted for and none overlooked. He stayed only for an hour or so, and then left on the next stage of his mission. He had requested the Japanese sergeant to accompany him to assist in tracing the camps. The sergeant's hand was shaken by many at Takli, and he beamed happiness.

About three hundred men arrived in the camp, having marched there from a working camp some miles north of Takli. Among them were Lionel and Ivan Newman, and others whom Ian had known at Wampo and Tamuang. They had left Tamuang days before the Takli party, and had been taken to dig a system of defensive tunnels for the Japanese infantry in central Thailand. Theirs had been very heavy work indeed, and their guards had driven hard and mercilessly. The tunnel entrances had to be dug underneath the roots of large trees so that they were easily concealed and protected.

An RAF pilot discussed with some men the nature of POW life and the Japanese threat to massacre POWs if the Allies invaded the territory in which they were held. He told them of the massacre of POWs in camps in North Borneo in October/November 1944 when the Australians landed there. Ron and Ian knew that their brother Malcolm had been moved to Borneo, and wondered.

All wanted to leave at the earliest opportunity, a fact which helped to maintain discipline, because those who fell foul of very sensible and modest rules would be punished by being pushed to the back of the queue. The MO advised all not to touch the Thai whiskey, known by the men as firewater. He warned that it was heavily laced with wood alcohol and could cause insanity, blindness or death. Ian was glad he had vomited it all up on that drunken orgy of his on Christmas Day 1943.

At last the day arrived when Ian, with his brother, were in a party due to be flown off if the weather permitted Dakotas to land. And it was a bright and clear morning, so they were justifiably confident. A plane landed and the lucky men were soon aboard a lorry on their way to the airstrip. Ten Japanese soldiers, former POW guards, stood to attention and bowed as the men were driven out of the camp gate. At the airstrip, the pilot and crew joined the group of happy men as they lined up in front of the Dakota to be photographed. And then they were on their way to Rangoon, the first leg of their journey home. As the plane passed over the railway the pilot told them that it could be seen out of port side windows, and dipped a wing to provide a better view. The men looked, but there was nothing said. It was not even impressive.

At Rangoon, they were received by a senior officer and taken to a canteen for refreshments. They were showered with gifts of cigarettes, chocolates – and handkerchiefs, for which many found an immediate use. Indeed, the tears which readily flooded the men's eyes and required mopping were replaced by more on each of the occasions when even the smallest acts of kindness were done to them. Even kind words on their own could cause eyes to well with tears.

They remained in Rangoon only briefly, because their return home had been given priority over all other servicemen due home for demobilisation. But during their few days in Rangoon they received generous and kind treatment by the servicemen there. Whether queuing at the services cinema – which was free – or at the canteen for meals, they were plucked out upon recognition as ex-POWs, and taken all the way to the front, whether they agreed or not. And they were easily recognised because they preferred shoes to boots and dressed comfortably, rather than in proper uniform which was hot in that climate. Woebetide any military policeman or any sergeant major or any officer who was insensitive enough to lay a finger on them!

And their subsequent treatment aboard troopships, their reception at the ports and railway stations, the greetings from VIPs, from everyone, overwhelmed them. And they still had the pleasure of the meetings and the greetings of their families and friends, which awaited them. They were happy men. Their ordeal was over.

Epilogue

IN DUE COURSE Ron and Ian met up with their father who had been a civilian internee in Singapore's Changi jail, and their mother and sister who had been evacuated to India. Their father was in not unreasonable health.

Their brother Malcolm did not return. A telegram from the War Office stated that he died in North Borneo on 30 November 1944, and that the cause of death was not known.

WARNING

GUARD YOUR TONGUE

YOU are free now. Anything you say in public or to the press is liable to be published throughout the whole world.

You have direct or indirect knowledge of the fate of many of your comrades who died in enemy hands as a result of brutality or neglect.

Your story, if published in the more sensational press, would cause much unnecessary unhappiness to relatives and friends.

If you had not been lucky enough to have survived and had died an unpleasant death at the hands of the Japanese, you would not have wished your family and friends to have been harrowed by lurid details of your death.

That is just what will happen to the families of your comrades who did die in that way if you start talking too freely about your experience.

It is felt certain that now you know the reason for this order you will take pains to spare the feelings of others.

Arrangements have been made for you to tell your story to interrogating officers who will then ask you to write it down.

You are not to say anything to anyone until after you have written out your statement and handed it in.

SPE/U/2

Appendix I

BUCKINGHAM PALACE

The Queen and I bid you a very warm welcome home.

Through all the great trials and sufferings which you have undergone at the hands of the Japanese, you and your comrades have been constantly in our thoughts. We know from the accounts we have already received how heavy those sufferings have been. We know also that these have been endured by you with the highest courage.

We mourn with you the deaths of so many of your gallant comrades.

With all our hearts, we hope that your return from captivity will bring you and your families a full measure of happiness, which you may long enjoy together.

George R.I.

September 1945.

Appendix 2